MW00523132

**SPEEDPRO SERIES**

# HOW TO POWER TUNE

# ALFA ROMEO

## TWIN-CAM ENGINES

### FOR ROAD & TRACK

# TO MY PARENTS

Other books of interest to enthusiasts available from Veloce -

*Alfa Romeo Owner's Bible*
    by Pat Braden
*Alfa Romeo Modello 8C 2300*
    by Angela Cherrett
*Alfa Romeo Giulia Coupe GT & GTA*
    by John Tipler
*Biggles!*
    by Peter Berresford Ellis
    & Jennifer Schofield
*Bubblecars & Microcars Colour Family Album*
    by Andrea & David Sparrow
*Bugatti 57 - The Last French Bugatti*
    by Barrie Price
*Car Bodywork & Interior: Care & Repair*
    by David Pollard
*Car Security Manual*
    by David Pollard
*Citroen 2CV Colour Family Album*
    by Andrea & David Sparrow
*Citroen DS Colour Family Album*
    by Andrea & David Sparrow
*Cobra - The Real Thing!*
    by Trevor Legate

*Completely Morgan: Four-Wheelers 1936 to 1968*
    by Ken Hill
*Completely Morgan: Four-Wheelers from 1968*
    by Ken Hill
*Fiat & Abarth 124 Spider & Coupe*
    by John Tipler
*Fiat & Abarth 500 & 600*
    by Malcolm Bobbitt
*How To Give Your MGB V-8 Power (SpeedPro Series)*
    by Roger Williams
*Lola T70*
    by John Starkey
*Mazda MX5/Miata Enthusiast's Workshop Manual*
    by Rod Grainger & Pete Shoemark
*Mini Cooper: The Real Thing!*
    by John Tipler
*Nuvolari: When Nuvolari Raced ...*
    by Valerio Moretti
*Pass the MoT*
    by David Pollard
*Rover P4*
    by Malcolm Bobbitt

First published in 1995 by Veloce Publishing Plc., Godmanstone, Dorset DT2 7AE, England. Fax 01300 341065

ISBN 1 874105 44 8

© Jim Kartalamakis and Veloce Publishing Plc 1995

Readers with ideas for automotive books, or books on other transport or related hobby subjects, are invited to write to the editorial director of Veloce Publishing at the above address.

British Library Cataloguing in Publication Data -
A catalogue record for this book is available from the British Library.

Typesetting (Soutane), design and page make-up all by Veloce on Apple Mac.

Cover pictures. The front panel photograph by David Sparrow features detail of David Hood's Rossi Engineering/Scuderia Britalia racing Alfa. Based on a '67 Sprint GTV and developed over many years., David's car is now very radical featuring a Twin Spark head on a standard block, tubular and rose-jointed suspension, rack & pinion steering and a, mainly, plastic body which is 6 inches wider than the GTA it resembles. Watch out for David's car in European classic motorsport. The rear panel photograph shows Rob Giordanelli's Scuderia Britalia car ahead of more modern opposition. This 105 series GTA lookalike and its driver have been very popular and successful in British motorsport. Essentially the car has a similar specification to David Hood's racer. (Photo courtesy of Rob Giordanelli).

Printed and bound in England.

SPEEDPRO SERIES

# HOW TO POWER TUNE
# ALFA ROMEO
## TWIN-CAM ENGINES
### FOR ROAD & TRACK

## Jim Kartalamakis

VELOCE PUBLISHING PLC
PUBLISHERS OF FINE AUTOMOTIVE BOOKS

# INTRODUCTION

There is something magical about the make of car known as Alfa Romeo.

Those who understand the history behind the Alfa they drive usually become enthusiasts because much of the marque's driveability and character is derived from racing and racing research; from winning, from losing and, sometimes, even from copying the best ideas of others. To those who really understand, the Alfa they drive is not just a piece of metal with a serial number and wheels: instead it's the continuation of a great tradition which evokes images of speed and excitement, names like Vittorio, Luigi and Giovanni, places like Portello, Arese, Balocco and Udine.

People who want to know everthing, and more, about their favorite marque and who want nothing from the knowledge but pleasure in this material world of ours, are known as "car enthusiasts," "car buffs," "*aficionados*," "car nuts" or plain "nuts." Personally, I accept any of these names, but prefer to be called an "*Alfista*": a term not only descriptive of the nature of my sickness but a grammatically plausible and correct statement.

We *Alfisti* are blessed with Alfa clubs which provide information on repairs, restoration and parts availability. We also have proprietary shop manuals and factory publications covering most aspects of most Alfa models. So far, so good. But what do we do if we want to improve the breed by extracting a bit more power from our already well-designed machines? Well, that's where I hope I can make a contribution to the world's stock of useful Alfa information.

With this small tribute to the four-cylinder Alfa, I have endeavored to present a step-by-step guide to improving the performance of Alfa's classic dohc engine. I hope I have expressed my ideas and related instructions clearly enough to make this book a pleasant and straightforward read, as well as a truly practical guide to performance modifications.

I extend my thanks to Rob Giordanelli and David Hood of Rossi Engineering. David was kind enough to read the whole manuscript and made many helpful suggestions. Both Rob and David made their racing Alfas available for photographic sessions.

Jim Kartalamakis
Athens, Greece.

# CONTENTS

# ESSENTIAL INFORMATION, USING THIS BOOK & TOOLKIT

## ESSENTIAL INFORMATION

This book contains information on practical procedures; however, this information is intended only for those with the qualifications, experience, tools and facilities to carry out the work in safety and with appropriately high levels of skill. Although the words **Warning!** (personal danger) and **Caution!** (danger of mechanical damage) are used throughout this book, be aware that we cannot possibly foresee every possibility of danger in every circumstance. Whenever working on a car or component, remember that your personal safety must **ALWAYS** be your **FIRST** consideration. **The publisher, author, editors and retailer of this book cannot accept any responsibility for personal injury or mechanical damage which results from using this book, even if caused by errors or omissions in the information given. If this disclaimer is unacceptable to you, please return the pristine book to your retailer who will refund the purchase price.**

This book applies to Alfa Romeo four-cylinder in-line double overhead camshaft engines (except Twin Spark and GTA) of capacities between 1300cc and 2000cc as used for the 101 series Giulietta onwards. The information given does not apply to Alfa Romeo flat-four, six-cylinder or Vee configuration engines.

Please be aware that changing component specification by modification is likely to void warranties and also to absolve manufacturers from any responsibility in the event of component failure and the consequences of such failure. It is also possible that changing the engine's specification will mean that it no longer complies with exhaust emission control regulations in your state or country - check before you start work. Increasing the engine's power will place additional stress on engine components and on the car's complete driveline: this may reduce service life and increase the frequency of breakdown. You need to know that varying production tolerances in cylinder head castings can mean that breakthrough to the waterways can occur if exhaust and intake tracts are enlarged. If such breakthrough does occur it's most likely that the head will have to be junked.

An increase in engine power and therefore performance will mean that your car's braking and suspension systems will need to be kept in perfect condition and uprated as appropriate.

## USING THIS BOOK

Throughout this book the text assumes that you or your contractor will have an appropriate Alfa Romeo workshop manual to follow for complete detail on dismantling, reassembly, adjustment procedure, clearances, torque figures, etc. This book's default is the standard Alfa Romeo specification for your model so, if a procedure is not described, a measurement not given, a torque figure ignored, you can assume that the standard procedure or specification for your car needs to be used.

You'll find it helpful to read the whole engine chapter (and preferably the whole book) before you start work or give instructions to your contractor. This is because a modification or change in specification in one area will cause the need for changes in other areas. Get the whole picture so that you can finalize specification and component requirements before any work begins.

As the Alfa Romeo was built to metric measurements, these take priority in the text. It is essential that you work with metric wrenches, but we would also advise you to use metric measurements if you can.

This book has been written in American English; those in any doubt over terminology will find a glossary of terms at the back of the book.

## TOOLKIT

Naturally, we embark on a series of modifications with the right tools at hand, which is to say, a set of combination box (ring) and open end metric wrenches, a socket and ratchet set, vise grip (Mole grip) pliers, screwdrivers, hammer (copper if possible), valve spring compressor, feeler gauges, torque wrench, inside spring loaded caliper, micrometer, vernier calipers, Plastigage strips and, finally, a drill gun (electric drill) with an assortment of rotary files and rotary emery bits from 60 to 320 grit.

A very welcome addition would be a high speed grinder capable of around 26-30,000rpm and of no less than 300 watts with a 6mm (0.25 inch) chuck.

Last, but not least, you must have an old pan in which to clean parts and another clean pan to hold cleaned parts. Use a proprietary cleaning fluid. If you can get hold of some liters, or gallons, of a chemical called MEK (for Methylethylketone) you will do a much, much better job. It removes dirt at a very fast rate and evaporates completely leaving no residue. Since it evaporates quickly, try to keep it covered up when not in use and please ensure adequate ventilation around your work area. Do not smoke in its presence and take all precautions applicable to other fuels. I've grown so accustomed to using MEK for cleaning engine parts that I won't use anything else. I think you will like the results too. **Warning!** Whatever specialist cleaning fluid you use, be sure to follow - completely - its manufacturer's instructions.

I cannot overstress the vital importance of cleaning a part before working on it, but I'm sure most of you believe in this practice anyway. And be sure that when I say clean, I mean brand new unused clean. There, I'm happy now!

If you insist on performing most of the work described yourself, you will have to have some simple special tools made up. I like to make such tools myself as I derive much satisfaction by having done something personally: also, I get to keep the tools and they surely will come in handy helping a friend someday.

# Chapter 1
# ENGINE

## BASIC DESCRIPTION OF ENGINE

The Alfa double overhead camshaft (dohc), or twin-cam, four-cylinder engine has its origins in the 'fifties. In its most common form it has sump, block and head made of an aluminium alloy. It features a forged steel crankshaft rotating in five main bearings and forged steel connecting rods. Four wet cylinder liners simplify serious repair work as they are virtually of the drop-in type. The cylinder head is one of the better parts of the engine, carrying two identical camshafts acting directly (*i.e.*: without pushrods) on the valves via bucket tappets.

Carburetion is (usually) by two double choke sidedraft carburettors and sometimes by mechanical or electronic indirect fuel injection. In 2000cc form the standard engine puts out up to 131 DIN horsepower on carbs.

### The bad news ...

Now, let's proceed with the bad news about the shortcomings of 'our' engine and, unfortunately, there are a lot (no disrespect meant to the designers).

It would make sense to start with the part of the engine where power is actually generated, that is, the cylinder head. First off, we have a combustion chamber with a rather large area, out of necessity, of course, which is not very conducive to keeping generated heat inside the chamber itself. The size of the valves and the central spark plug (almost central, that is) dictates a large dome with a consequently large angle between the valves, all of 80 degrees. This, of course, is an improvement over the 90 degrees of years past. This large valve angle, and the decision to locate the intake and exhaust systems where they are, made for a much less than perfect arrangement of the intake and exhaust tracts within the head casting. Somehow, in this big dent called a combustion chamber, we must burn air and fuel and, to do this efficiently, we must first compress the resulting gas mixture. Unfortunately to create a reasonable compression ratio we have to fill up part of the dome with an aluminium alloy lump called a piston. The shape left empty when the piston reaches the top of its stroke (Top Dead Centre/TDC) is exactly like that of a super-large contact lens. Too bad, as we would really like the bottom of the space (i.e. the top of the piston) to be as flat as possible.

So far so good, or should I say so far so bad, since we are dealing with the shortcomings of our engine?

Let's continue on down to the cylinder block and cast a critical eye over it. Nice things those liners, but not very reliable under extreme conditions like racing. It would be nicer, much, much nicer if we could have a set of four in one piece wouldn't it? Very rare, I'm afraid.

A limiting factor to power poten-

1/1 Good and tried 105 series 2000cc engine, here being lowered into a Spider's engine bay.

1/2 Cutaway view of Spica-injected 2000cc 116 series engine. The Spica system was an excellent design which allowed Alfa Romeo to continue selling its '50s-designed dohc unit in the USA when emission controls began to bite.

tial is the long stroke of these engines. You can only make a rotating assembly turn so fast before pieces start flying off. Things like pistons and connecting rods. Power produced is proportional to engine speed (expressed as Revs Per Minute/RPM), provided the engine's breathing and mechanical limitations are not exceeded. For the 2000 engine, and the 1750 for that matter, we must be happy with a maximum of 6500-6700rpm for a well built motor with standard parts. The works GTAm cars were turning up to 7800rpm and the 16-valve 2000 at 8200rpm However, you can all guess how much these engines had in common with their cheaper relatives lurking under our hoods ...

### The good news ...

This much bad talk is not very helpful to our egos, so let's go on to point out the highlights of our motor. Notice that I stick to and am a firm believer in "first the bad news then the good news" because this leaves you at least a bit happier when it's over than you would be if things were put the other way around!

Starting off at the head once again, we find an excellent system of valve actuation, using tappets (or followers) with shims to adjust individual valve clearance. This system has the lowest possible reciprocating weight and so gives the potential to use radical cam designs with steep acceleration ramps. Granted with Alfa's valve actuation design adjusting clearances is somewhat difficult and time consuming but, once done properly, they stay correct for a long time.

Second on the advantages list is the fact that we have the freedom to set the intake and exhaust camshafts separately (relative to the crankshaft)

1/3 Cutaway view of the classic Alfa Romeo 2000 twin cam engine as used in the Giulia Veloce models.

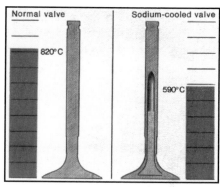

1/4 Illustration shows that sodium-filled valve stays much cooler than a conventional solid valve.

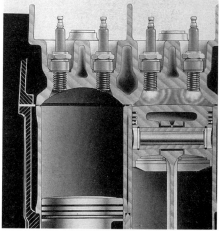

1/5 This is how the combustion area of the TS engine looks. Notice flat-top (almost) piston and compact combustion chamber. Plugs are upright, in contrast with GTA and GTAm designs.

to obtain different characteristics from our car than those the factory intended for us. Moving a bit lower, we find an almost centrally located spark plug which properly ignites the combustible mixture without excessive spark advance. Lower down inside the block, we have a very strong crankshaft and equally well built, but not excessively heavy, connecting rods. Fortunately the rod bolts are also of high quality, a very important point.

We have been blessed with large oil pans (or sumps, if you will) and finned at that, helping to keep oil temperatures within bounds.

Going back up to the head for a while, we check the valves and find that their shape is very good ( though not the best) and their size under the space limitations in the chamber is near the optimum mark. To top things off, the exhaust valve is sodium filled for better heat transfer and longer life. The double chain driving the valve gear has proven to be a strong component and accurate in its mission if a bit noisy (but we all love this kind of noise, don't we?).

It would be interesting to discuss, even if academically, how the factory could improve the current design of the engine which, as we have just seen, could stand a change for the better in some areas. Ergo, the 2000 Twin-Spark and its smaller derivatives the 1.7 and 1.8TS power units. These engines have been given a dose of the good ol' stuff including a twin ignition cylinder head. Much has been improved in the combustion chamber design. Very interesting is the reduction in valve angle from 80 to 46 degrees and the resultant improvement with better intake and exhaust

ignition and almost flat-top pistons, we can say for sure that the Twin Spark has a greater potential for tuning than the older motor.

The Twin Spark burns fuel more efficiently in a more compact chamber, thus it can produce more power as evidenced by its 148bhp at 5800rpm. The necessity of using two plugs per cylinder was brought about by the requirement for a reduction in valve angle. The valves are closer together now and there simply is no room to fit a central plug. Putting a single plug to one side would make for uneven burning characteristics and, possibly, necessitate a higher advance curve because of the longer flame travel path. However, by duplicating the spark plug on the other side of the chamber we shorten flame travel,

**1/7 Below: 1.8IE (1779cc) engine for the Alfa 75. With its Bosch Motronic engine management system, this engine's good for 122bhp.**

**1/6 The intake system of this 2000TS (Twin Spark) experimental engine, contained an array of reed-valves aimed at increasing torque while detracting only 1 or 2 horsepower from maximum power. This scheme, however, never made it to the showrooms.**

port geometry. Valve head sizes for the 2000 unit are 44 intake and 38mm exhaust respectively. By comparison the 105 series 2000 engine's exhaust valves are of 40mm but let me point out to the not so well informed that the GTAm had 46.5 and 38mm valves - kind of rings a bell, doesn't it! On the other hand, the old and revered GTAs had 45 and 41mm intakes and ex-hausts - an obvious error exhaust-wise, especially when coupled to 34mm I.D. (Inside Diameter) headers (exhaust manifolds). Therefore, with its revised head design, correct valve sizes, two plugs per cylinder for better

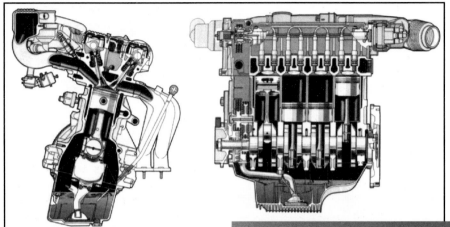

1/8 Left: cross-sections of 164 2000TS engine.

1/10 Formula 3 development of 2000TS engine by the Pedrazzani brothers of Novara. This engine has several important differences from the production unit: single rear distributor, external toothed drivebelt to single top pulley which, in turn, drives cams via two internal gears, bore 87mm and stroke 84mm, titanium connecting rods and much more, for an output power of 165bhp at 5500rpm while breathing through a 24mm restrictor air box (class rules).

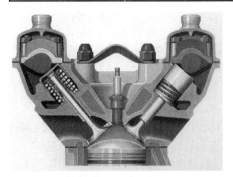

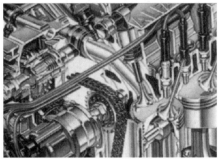

1/9a & b Close-up cutaways reveal 2000TS engine's better port geometry than single plug twin cam engine (top).

decrease advance requirements, achieve better ignition altogether and can use domed pistons for higher-still compressions in racing without all the disadvantages of an 'orange peel' combustion chamber. Add to all this the capacity to fit very large valves, and there you have it: the true potential of the new GTA type head. Using two distributors, one in the normal place and one driven off the exhaust cam, takes care of spark requirements. To increase low speed torque the new car even has a variable intake cam timing system, electronically controlled, of course.

One may wonder, not without reason, how the new engine manages to keep proper advance characteristics using two different distributors? In this age of Bosch Motronic engine management systems, the two distributors are doing just that: distributing high voltage: all else being taken care of electronically by microprocessor. In F3 guise, this engine uses a single distributor driven off the intake camshaft.

Gentlemen, hats off to Alfa one more time! This is what is meant by 'state of the art'. It's the technology that keeps Alfa winning on the racetracks of the world.

In the past, Alfa has used a 16-valve head in the racing Alfettas and, despite considerable experience with the design, decided not to offer it as a production option, even though competitors are doing so: Fiat, VW, BMW, Mercedes, Toyota, Saab, Peugeot. We, as enthusiasts, would like nothing better than to have a bolt-on monster for our cars but, alas, it hasn't happened so far. The factory's answer to the competition was the variable intake timing system which offered higher torque low down without decreasing power at the top end of the rev range. Low and mid-range torque has always been the strong point of Alfas and they were not about to relinquish this established feature. As you may well know, low range torque is not something people with 16V motors like to talk about. This is a fact proven many times in road tests of the same cars with 8V and 16V engines. The results are always typical. Lower down the range the 8 valves have better acceleration and higher up the 16 valves take over.

Now, potential horsepower is something else. Sixteen valves usually rule in racing, but no one is driving the racing car in town. Alfa looked at it this way, that way, and decided to go with two plugs thus retaining and increasing low speed torque without affecting the high range. As a matter of fact, I believe that using 8 sparkplugs has no

disadvantage at all! The fact that the 75 twin spark has 'only' 148bhp DIN at 5800rpm tells me that it's a wolf in sheep's clothing. The potential is there and that's important.

Possibly, the thought of having in-house model conflicts did not appeal to Alfa's brass. It wouldn't look right having the top sports model, the GTV, with six cylinders and 158 horsepower, and the four-door model with four cylinders and more power. They must have thought of this, because along with the 75TS they announced that the 2.5-litre. engine has been brought up to 3-litres.

Nice as all this may be, I believe that there is nothing a true *Alfista* would like more than a Montreal engine in a GTV! Dreams sometimes come true, but not often and only for a special purpose.

The dream here is, of course, the Group 5 Alfettas campaigned in the 'seventies. 22 GTV-V8s were made with their Montreal engines resized to 2800cc.

On the other hand, most true enthusiasts like to keep their cars mostly in original specification with, if possible, increased power from the original engine. Whether you're modifying your original engine, or a bigger one to fit in the old engine bay, I hope to provide you with real help

### What you can do
You will be able to do a great deal of the work described in this book yourself. Depending on your experience and confidence, there are some jobs where you'll have to make the decision between do it yourself or getting a machine shop to do it. Lastly a small number of the tasks can be done only by a machine shop. However, you must ensure that when work goes to a machine shop, it is done exactly to your specifications.

## BASIC AREAS TO IMPROVE

Unless otherwise stated, this book uses the 105 engine in all its forms as the basis of descriptions. When sizes and measurements are quoted without reference to a particular engine size, they will apply to the 2000 which is used as a default as this engine seems to be the most popular amongst *Alfisti*

**1/11 Alfa experimented with two (left), three (centre), and four-valve (right) heads before marketing the two valve TS item. Strange-looking device in center is the experimental reed-valve which never made it to production.**

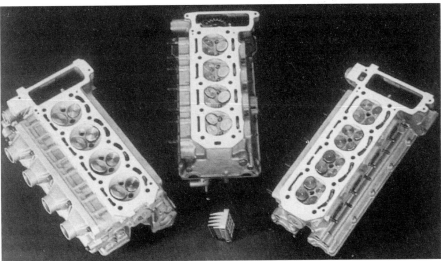

searching for more power. However, where required, data covering other engine sizes is included.

Let's see which areas can be modified with increased performance and reliability in mind. We can work on the engine's breathing system which offers the highest gains in power without using any special parts. Unfortunately, it's the area that will cost us the most in time and effort, too, but the results will be worth it. By the term 'breathing system', I mean everything over the block and not just the cylinder head. It starts at the mouth of the air filter box and ends at the tailpipe - chrome or not. Improving the engine's breathing will take up most of our time, and will be followed by cylinder block work, building procedures, oil system modifications and then by my favorite subject: camshafts.

1/12 Combustion chamber view of modified 2000cc cylinder head with oversize valve seat inserts installed. In this particular head, 46mm intake valves were installed, and intake port dimensions were modified accordingly.

## THE PROJECT ENGINE

Carrying out the modifications described in this book will enable you to build a 2000 engine with around 165bhp at the flywheel, produced at a modest 6500-6700rpm The car will be entirely suitable for town driving, with no jerks, kinks or coughing. I would even go so far as to call it economical by fast car standards. Performing the same type of modifications to the smaller capacity engines should result in about 120bhp for the 1300, 140bhp for the 1600 and 155bhp for the 1750/1800 engine.

You might like to know that 2000 engines can be installed in any model of 105/115 series car with minimal problems, though if the donor car is a 116 series model you'll probably have to do some swapping of oil pans and flywheels. You'll also need to swap the water pump to get the necessary tacho drive.

## CYLINDER HEAD

### Cylinder head & intake manifold - optimizing air flow

What the cylinder head tracts do is allow the flow of the required air/fuel mixture into the cylinders and the exhaust gases out. Intake flow results from the vacuum created in the cylinder by the descending piston and exhaust flow from the rising piston and partly by gas pressure: we must strive to remove all possible obstacles in the way of good air flow.

By using instruments known as flow-benches, air flow into and out of an engine can be measured and the value of modifications to the intake and exhaust tracts assessed. Large flow benches can also be used to evaluate air filters, exhaust headers, silencers and everything else where good gas flow is important to performance. Coming up with guidance on

how and where to modify heads is a painstaking procedure, involving many hours of trial and error work with constant flow-bench measurements. It is more than usual to destroy a couple of heads before being able to visualize how a good tract, conducive to high flow, should look. This painstaking work on intake and exhaust tracts can then be coupled to measurements taken with different shapes of valve at various lifts until optimum results are achieved. In this way an improvement over what the factory has given you can be obtained but, do not, even for a moment, assume that the manufacturer doesn't know how to improve the heads it makes. What it boils down to are economic considerations and an understandable reluctance to over design a product and therefore build in more manufacturing time and cost. Alfa heads, as they come from the factory, flow very respectably- better

**1/13 Truly a sight for sore eyes!** Bottom view of the GTAm cylinder head. Note integral intake manifold with studs and the separate "adaptor manifold" which permitted use of Weber 45 DCOE carbs for an output power of 200bhp at 7000rpm. GTAm engines in this configuration were used in rally Alfetta GTs in place of the 16-valve engine: the latter was almost useless below 4000rpm, but capable of about 245bhp at around 8000rpm! The true potential of the 16-valve engine was never exploited, as development was cut short. Few of these units were produced, all using the "guillotine" throttle slide assembly and airbox (both of GTAm origin). Like the GTAm, this engine used a one-piece (monosleeve) liner.

than a lot of other maker's.

I have experimented to see how much more a modified Alfa dohc head can flow and using the 2000 head for my work because: a) it will yield more power than its smaller capacity counterparts and b) I had something almost perfect with which to compare it - a GTAm head (1985cc, twin-plug). Using the GTAm as a target standard, and applying all I have learned from the masters of the trade (like Vizard, Wilson, Yunick, Bell), various professionally modified race engines and my own experience, I have carried out a series of experimental modifications to standard Alfa dohc heads.

My experiments have resulted in two stages of head modification: the first stage offers a sizeable flow increase over the standard head (about 14%) but retains the standard valves; stage two goes further and increases flow by 25% above standard by using 46mm valves and appropriate valve seat inserts. I must say that these modifications provide very satisfactory power gains: a standard valve (stage one) engine with 12mm, 300 degree cams, 11.8:1 compression ratio, 2x45 DCOE, Asso 7003 pistons, 4 into 1 open exhaust and running on AVGAS showed 192bhp at 7100rpm on the dyno. This engine was subsequently installed in a road-going Giulia GT 2000 Coupe and the car was FAST! The only further modifications needed were a lower advance curve (necessitated by low octane pump fuels) and a specially fabricated 4-2-1 exhaust system. Final note: it idles perfectly at just 900rpm!

Power from the big-valve head (stage two) has not been measured on a dyno so far but, judging from the flow-bench data, we should be looking at something around 205-215bhp. I base this figure on the fact that the carbureted GTAm - yes, they were used in rally prepared Alfettas - produced 200bhp at 7000rpm. A comparable head (flow-wise) with state of the art cams should make a bit more power. As a thought, consider the Alfa Novamotor Formula 3 Twin-Spark engine which developed 167bhp at 6000rpm with a 24mm airbox restrictor intake.

As far as the big valves in the stage two head are concerned, they are special parts available from Italy (Autotrasformazioni Gozzoli - Maranello). Their shape is optimized and they have 8mm valve stems necessitating use of suitable 8mm guides that fit (from BMW) as well as appropriate seals. If you want to take the big valve route, you'll have to install larger valve seat inserts with an O.D. of 46.5mm (1.830in). Cast iron is good enough if you have access to leaded fuel. For a perfect job, have the inserts made of special bronze for durability and improved heat transfer. Oh, by the way, the large valves have 45 degree seats instead of 30 degree, which further enhances flow. Valve clearance adjustment can be carried out with the regular 9mm shims - don't worry, they won't fall off!

Regarding exhaust valves, it seems that the standard items are adequate for our 'Project Engine' (30 degree seats and all!) but use genuine Alfa parts -ATE, TRW or Livia - as there are lookalikes on the market which are not sodium-filled (the

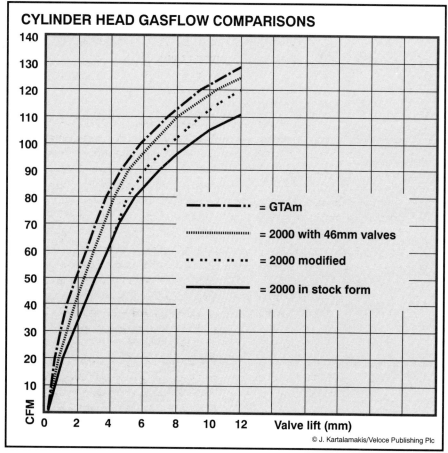

## CYLINDER HEAD GASFLOW COMPARISONS

-·-·-· = GTAm

·············· = 2000 with 46mm valves

·- ·- ·- ·· = 2000 modified

——— = 2000 in stock form

© J. Kartalamakis/Veloce Publishing Plc

**1/14 Comparison flow-bench results for various heads. Note the great flow increase given by 46mm valves. GTAm engine also uses 46mm valves, but with steeper inlet tracts. The modified 2000 head was modified as detailed in the text.**

basic formula is that the increase in CFM (flow in Cubic Feet per Minute) multiplied by a factor of 0.43 equals the power increase in bhp. As an example, if you increase your cylinder head's flow rate by 15CFM then power will increase by 6.45bhp.

Some of you may have wondered about fitting a modern Twin Spark cylinder head to an older block as a shortcut to higher performance. Well, the good news is that it can be done, the bad news that you need to be a seriously good engineer - and have a well-stuffed pocketbook - to achieve the modification. David Hood of Team Britalia, who is associated with Rossi Engineering in the UK, has successfully undertaken such a transplant and has 'seen' 220bhp at 7000rpm from his seriously modified 2100cc racing engine. David believes there is much more to come with further development. One other point to note is that the TS block is considerably stronger than earlier units, so you'd be better off to consider a full engine transplant.

**Cylinder head - preparation**

I'll begin by making a couple of reasonable assumptions: 1), you've separated the head from the rest of the engine, and 2), you've cleaned away oil and old gasket material.

After removing the valve spring retainers, keepers, springs and bases clean these parts and put them in a box so that you'll know where they

sodium filling is a definite cooling advantage). Alternatively, for those seeking maximum performance and/or an engine more likely to survive, go for aftermarket modern solid valves made especially for high performance engines. Modern metallurgy makes such valves good at heat dissipation (their manufacturers may suggest you use special guides) and they have the advantage that they only bend in the event of piston contact (sodium filled valves tend to lose their heads in the same situation, a problem which can cause a great deal of damage).

Take a look at the comparative head intake flow graph (1/14).

Superflow have come up with a formula which shows the power increase you can expect from cylinder head gas flow improvements (assuming the flow is not impeded by intake and exhaust system limitations). The

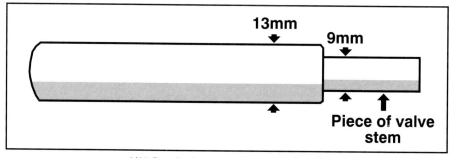

**13mm**

**9mm**

**Piece of valve stem**

**1/15 Detail of valve guide removal tool.**

are a few weeks down the road. There is no need to number any of the items removed.

Now, turn your attention to the valve guides. They may have served you well and faithfully so far, but they are an obstacle to port shaping and will need to be modified too: this cannot be done in their natural habitat. Some further justification for valve guide removal is that they're probably worn.

To remove the old guides you will have to work from the outside in, in other words, they will have to be pushed out towards the combustion chamber. You will need to use a copper-headed hammer and a suitable punch like the one illustrated (1/15). You'll be really surprised at how easy it is to drive out the valve guides. While hammering, take care not to damage the rest of the head. Discard the old guides when you have taken them out, unless you prefer to practice guide modification on them before carrying out the real work on new guides.

You are now ready to begin decarbonizing the chambers and the intake and exhaust tracts. Fit a wire brush attachment to a drill gun (electric drill) and get ready for action, including the wearing of appropriate protective gear. This job will prove to be dirty with old soot flying about so, if you can, do it outside. Start scrubbing, but be careful: you can easily scratch the alloy chamber walls. I have found that a cup-shaped wire brush of around 38mm (1.5 inches) diameter does an excellent job of cleaning chambers, especially around projecting valve seat lips where the deposits are very hard.

Having dealt with the chambers, turn your attention to the eight intake and exhaust tracts. The drill gun will be used here too, but with another

attachment: a wire brush with radial whiskers of about 25mm (1-1.5 inches) in diameter. This job is a dirty one too, especially in the exhaust tracts: there's usually a lot of soot to be removed here.

After wire brushing the breathing tracts, clean the whole head with a proprietary solvent, especially around the valve seats and inside the spark plug threads. Now is the time to check for cracks and their extent. Cracks usually form from the valve seat inserts to the inside of the spark plug hole. Do not be alarmed by small cracks, they are not deep enough to threaten you. Be concerned by cracks that seem deep, or small pieces of alloy missing next to the valve seats. If you are not sure about how bad the cracks are, take the head to your trusted Alfa dealer, engineering shop or knowledgeable friend for professional advice. I should point out that there are very few used Alfa dohc heads without any cracks at all and, fortunately, most such cracks are harmless.

Next, check the valve seat inserts. A little pitting is acceptable but large pits are not and, certainly, no cracks are allowed. It is very important that the working surface of the seat insert is not, I repeat, *not* sunk below the wall of the combustion chamber. If any inserts are sunk, it's the result of an overly savage refacing job: such inserts must be replaced or a replacement head in better condition found.

While on the subject of valve seat inserts, observe those strange cut-outs in the 2000 chamber which do not exist in any other head. The valves in the 2000 engine are rather large so these cutouts unshroud the valves and facilitate better breathing. Do not smooth out these cutouts, no modifications are necessary in the combustion chamber except perhaps a little polishing; that only if you feel like it.

You will notice at this point that the extreme outside edge of the valve seat inserts forms a little lip extending inside the chamber. The lip will have to go, however, we'll return to valve seats later.

### Intake tracts - modification

At this point, our main and immediate task is to shape the intake and exhaust tracts for increased flow. Here, when I refer to intake tracts I'm including the intake manifold also. Now's the time to get hold of a decent intake manifold of carburetor type and, preferably, from a large Alfa dohc engine. The reason for this is that 1750 and 2000 manifolds have larger bores which means less metal to remove.

Clean the intake manifold as well as you can. It's important to know what you have at hand, and where you want to go to achieve the results you want. I submit to your scrutiny the "before and after" diagrams (1/16 & 1/17) of an intake manifold and cylinder head (2000 model) that is, the stock items and the modified items. Stock (standard) sizes shown may vary by one half to one millimeter (0.020-0.040in) due to different casting moulds used and even tiny year-to-year variations. For example, late Alfetta heads have smaller ports in general than Berlina 1973 heads. If you want to determine the approximate year a head was made, look at the back of the head, the part facing the firewall (bulkhead). There is a number there, a two digit number. By comparing that number with another located on a head with a known fabrication year (the year of the car it's in) you will know whether it's older or newer. For example, the "35" head belongs in the late '80s as far as casting goes.

Back to business now. You'll notice that the modified intake mani-

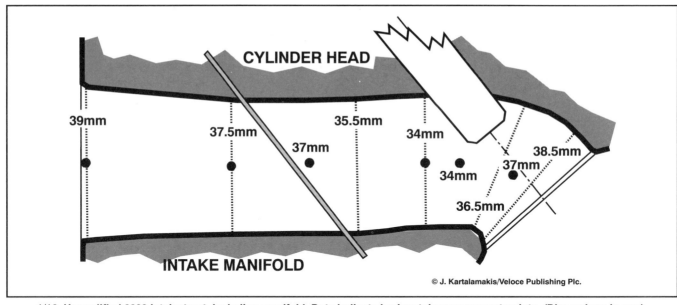

**1/16  Unmodified 2000 intake tract, including manifold. Dots indicate horizontal measurement points. (Dimensions in mm).**

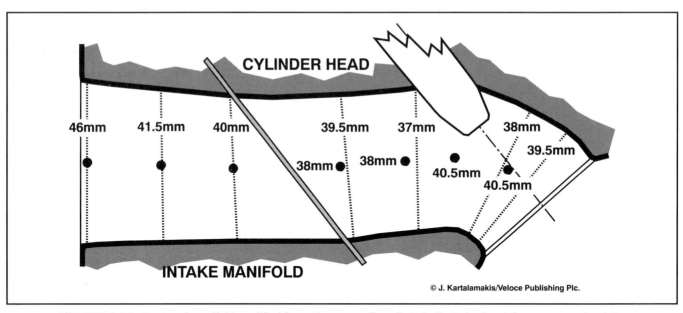

**1/17  2000 intake tract and manifold modified for optimum gas flow. Dots indicate horizontal measurement points. (Dimensions in mm).**

fold (1/17) is bored out to accept 45mm carbs in the case of 2000cc engines. I believe this to be a very sound move toward higher power from the Alfa twin-cam engine and there are no serious drawbacks. Even if you don't have any 45 carbs just now 40mm carbs will work just as well up to about 150 horsepower, and probably better up to 3500rpm or so. Don't worry about the mismatch between a 40mm carb or mounting block and a 45mm manifold. You won't know it's there in terms of engine performance. Later on, when you get your hands on a pair of 45s just bolt them on, assuming the rubber blocks are 45mm also.

For those of you modifying the smaller Alfa engines, refer to the diagram (1/18) and aim for the following intake tract dimensions with a smooth transition from dimension to dimension along the tract -

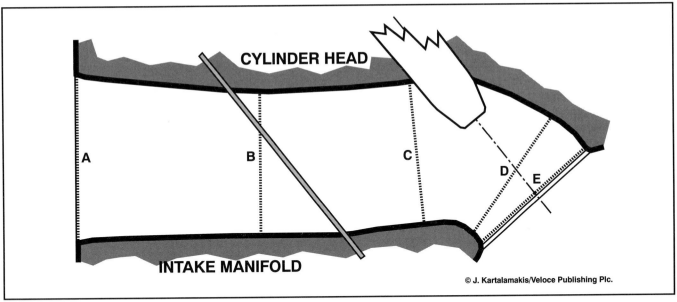

CYLINDER HEAD

A  B  C  D  E

INTAKE MANIFOLD

© J. Kartalamakis/Veloce Publishing Plc.

**1/18 Modified intake tract, including manifold, for 1300 to '1800' engines. See text for relevant dimensions.**

| Engine | 1300 | 1600 | 1750/<br>1800 |
|---|---|---|---|
| *Dimension A* | *41mm* | *41mm* | *46mm* |
| *Dimension B* | *36mm* | *37mm* | *40mm* |
| *Dimension C* | *32mm* | *34mm* | *36mm* |
| *Dimension D* | *34mm* | *37mm* | *37mm* |

There is a fair amount of grinding to do in the intake tract and I suggest that you tackle it with an open mind, a lot of patience and with careful and constant reference to the relevant drawings. Alternatively, if you have doubts about your abilities, you may wish to entrust the work to a specialist. Whichever, work starts on any one of the four intake ports in the head, but concentrate on the rough grinding first. **Caution!** Care really is of paramount importance here as the odd inadvertent over-use of the cutter may cause a breakthrough to the water jacket. Note that in some areas, for example around the guide boss, there is no room for mistakes as you are - literally - cutting it close. Another area not to make mistakes in is the part between the guide boss and the valve seat insert.

Rotary files and cutters clog up quickly on aluminum so you must keep them lubricated with a 50/50 mixture of fuel oil and paraffin. You'll then find that your cutters don't clog up any more and metal is removed at a faster rate.

During the rough cutting, constantly check the diameter of what you are cutting by using spring loaded inside calipers. Adjust the caliper setscrew until the caliper tips just touch the walls of the port. Withdraw the calipers and measure the diameter with vernier calipers or by placing the inside calipers' tips next to a ruler. By this method you can measure how your work progresses until you have come to within half a millimeter (0.020in) of the desired size. While

**1/19 Cross section of 2000 (105) cylinder head. Pen lines on casting show how intake and exhaust tracts should be enlarged. Note how close to the water jacket you'll be grinding - take care! (Note: holes in tract walls were made to check wall thickness on this throwaway head).**

grinding, try to give the work a uniform finish with no lumps or rough spots. Do not grind any metal away from the short side exit to the valve seat insert that is directly opposite the valve guide. Here, maintain as large a radius as is possible because it is too sharp a bend as it comes from the factory anyway.

When the first cylinder head tract is roughly done, take a good look at the measurements at all points noted in the diagrams, and hopefully you will be just a bit short of them. You can see the general shape now and can appreciate the difference in area you have just produced. If you are doing this for the first time, the work just described will require about 2 to 3 hours. Now's the time to bolt on the intake manifold. Cut a few pieces off the old intake manifold gasket and place them on the head studs, then bolt on the manifold. Do this to allow for the gasket thickness effect, as the port holes would not completely line-up if the work were performed without this trick.

With the intake manifold bolted onto the head, grind away the metal in the manifold's tract (the same one as you've been working on in the head) until you get really close to the dimensions shown in the relevant diagram (1/17 or 1/18). This part of the work should take you another half hour.

Note that to facilitate work on the intake manifold, you can use a 45mm carb mounting block to scribe a line on the manifold outer face. Use this line as a guide to metal removal, and go about 0.5mm (0.020in) beyond it, to compensate for production tolerances.

Repeat the whole process on the other three tracts, using the same great patience and care. Every now and then, sit back and look at what you've done so far. I'm sure you'll start to realize that "something good is cook-

1/20 Genuine 45mm carb mounts are not very easy to find today. However, 40mm blocks can be modified with equally good results. Don't forget to enlarge paper gasket bores!

1/21 Clean, straight-through view of enlarged tracts. This modified head looks the business and delivers too, as evidenced from the flow bench graph elsewhere in these pages.

ing here". It's always heartening to take a look at progress being made and how much closer you are to what you're after.

Having rough-finished all intake tracts in the head and manifold you are ready to apply the final finish to them. By now the manifold and head joint should be hardly discernible (remember to use the old gaskets as spacers) and only visible as a dark

line. If this is the case, fit the emery rotary bit to the drill gun and attack the previously roughened work. You should derive great satisfaction from seeing the very smooth contours produced by the emery bits.

Move the emery bit in and out constantly, applying pressure judiciously at the same time against the walls of the tract. Start with a number 60 grit and proceed to 120, 240 and finally 320 grit. At this stage you should have a beautifully finished tract, not polished nor shining but, nevertheless, beautifully finished. This kind of finish is all that is required. Mirror finishing does nothing to help fuel atomization and proves detrimental to low rpm work. After all, we are building an engine for all-round use.

Incidentally, you may find that you cannot reach deep inside an intake tract at some point. In this case you'll have to separate the manifold from the head and then continue finishing the head part of the tracts.

When you think you have finished all intake tract work, take a final set of careful measurements everywhere. Congratulate yourself if you have four almost identical ports, with measurements matching those of the relevant diagrams (1/17 or 1/18). You may have to do a little repeat work to achieve the ideal dimensions but, once you reach the goal about 60 percent of the head work is complete!. I'm sure you've noticed that we haven't tackled any of the actual valve seat work yet, but that comes a little later.

Clean all intake tracts with a rag and separate the head from the manifold. Sandwich a new gasket between the two (no need to clamp the parts together), and scribe the larger size of the modified tracts around the protruding gasket edges inside the joint. Remove the gasket and carefully cut away the now excess material to 2mm (0.080in) *outside* the scribe marks.

## Exhaust tracts - modification

Now turn your attention to the exhaust tracts in the head. If they looked small before, compared to the stock intakes, they look even smaller now don't they? Well, after about another five hours of work you should have four

exhaust ports to be proud of!

A very important consideration when modifying exhaust tracts is the type of manifold which will be used. If you intend using an after-market header type (tubular steel manifold) unit, you MUST have it at hand when working on the exhaust tracts. There must be a correct relationship between each exhaust tract port and the corresponding header port. Notice I'm not referring to matching here, because it's not what we want in the strict sense of the word. Matching is out, and here's why -

In recent years it has been shown that if a restriction is created in the exhaust system near the valve, a one-way restriction at that, much of the exhaust gas backwash into the combustion chamber can be avoided. The re-entry of spent combustion products dilutes the fresh mixture and takes up precious space inside the chamber. This phenomenon becomes more pronounced as cam timing is altered for more power; it can even get so bad that it completely wipes out a well built motor at low rpm. Backwash is made worse by the use of large diameter header pipes, where gas velocities are lower. However, we must have a decent pipe diameter for higher rpm use.

Traditionally, it has been accepted that if you modify your engine for high rpm use, you can forget about the lower end of the scale. And so it was. Enter here the anti-reversion technique which says that by leaving a small step on the way *back* into the head, you can help out lower range performance. Well, anti-reversion is not really quite this simple but the general idea is. In other words, if, say, you have a 38mm header primary pipe, you enlarge the exhaust port to no more than 35mm, thus leaving a 1.5mm (0.060in) lip all around the

circumference. So, rest assured, matching the head and manifold exhaust ports completely would not bring any noticeable gain anywhere, but you would know the loss after having fitted a high-power cam.

If you plan to use the factory exhaust manifold - and only the European unit is considered here - you can chamfer (*i.e.* enlarge) the first 3mm (0.120in) of cast iron to create a step of 1.5mm (0.060in). However, I strongly discourage use of this manifold for two reasons. One is the ever present and almost, I'm afraid, certain chance of breakage and the second reason is to do with geometric considerations: wrong runner lengths (unequal at that), wrong four into two joints and wrong outlet diameters. We shall return to talk about exhaust manifolds later.

Let's see how we modify the exhaust tracts in the cylinder head. The same method is followed here as with the intakes. First you rough out the port to within half to one millimeter of the finished size. Try to obtain as smooth a contour as possible with the cutter in order to minimize work with the emery bits later. You can appreciate that the amount of metal removed here is really quite a lot. This should tell you something about the potential of this engine and how underpowered it really is in stock form. To really make a point here, suffice it to say that the exhaust port (2000) should be 38mm in diameter at the manifold surface, and it comes all of 33mm from the factory. And this is only for 5600rpm and a mild camshaft mind you! Kind of small, right?

Dimensions for a modified 2000 exhaust tract are shown in the diagram (1/22). Those modifying the exhaust tracts of smaller Alfa engines should also refer to the diagram (1/22) and the following dimensions table -

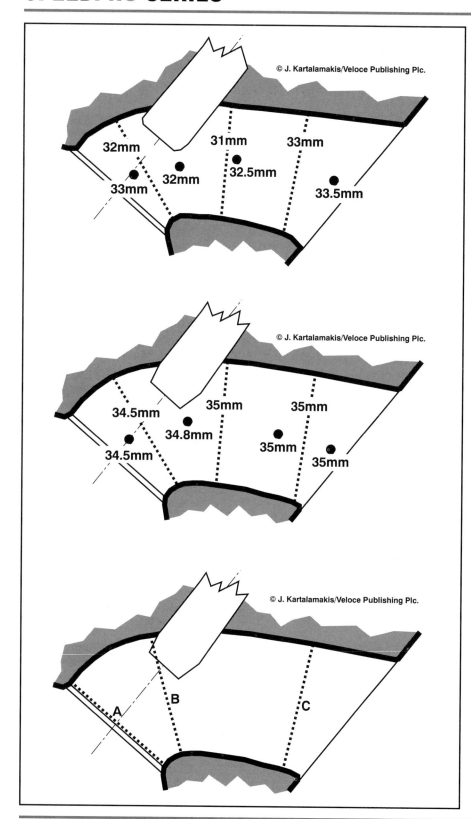

© J. Kartalamakis/Veloce Publishing Plc.

32mm

31mm       33mm

32mm

32.5mm

33mm

33.5mm

© J. Kartalamakis/Veloce Publishing Plc.

34.5mm

35mm      35mm

34.8mm

35mm

34.5mm

35mm

© J. Kartalamakis/Veloce Publishing Plc.

A    B      C

**1/22 Left: Three versions of the exhaust tract. Top, 2000 unmodified. Centre, 2000 modified for optimum gas flow. Bottom modification guide for 1300 to '1800' engines (key to dimensions in text). Note that dots show horizontal measurement points and that dimensions are in mm.**

| Engine | 1300 | 1600 | 1750/ 1800 |
|---|---|---|---|
| Dimension A | 30mm | 33mm | 33mm |
| Dimension B | 32mm | 32mm | 32mm |
| Dimension C | 33mm | 33mm | 33mm |

After consulting the relevant diagrams, fit a cutter (rotary file) to the drill chuck and attack the walls of an exhaust tract. You'll see that the narrowest of each tract is just around the valve guide boss. Fortunately, this area can be attacked from either end of the tract, whichever is convenient at any time. Measure your progress with internal calipers, as described earlier. One small, probably unnecessary, note here: don't attempt to work on the valve seat inserts with the cutter, it won't work. Modification of seats requires the use of small stones and rotary emery bits.

While you are working, every once in a while feel the inside of the tract with your fingers: there should be no 'hills' however small or other protuberances and the metal should feel dead smooth to the touch. Here again, take care not to work excessively on the short side radius of the port near the valve seat insert. Leave as large a radius as possible. The ports are shallow enough as it is, do not make them any worse.

Once you have the exhaust tracts in the head roughly finished the next step is to smooth them out with progressively finer emery bits. In contrast to the intake ports, here you should strive to obtain a polished-looking finish because, in this way, the

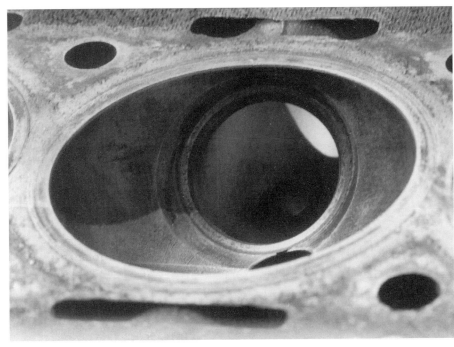

**1/23 Modified exhaust tract (2000). Looks huge, doesn't it?**

build-up of soot and other combustion by-products will be greatly retarded as there will be no rough surface for deposits to cling to.

### Cam follower bores - modification

Time now for a necessary modification. A high lift cam with large lobes will not be able to rotate in the stock head because the noses of the lobes will foul the tops of the follower bores! You have to form cut-outs to enable the cam lobes to rotate without obstruction. A flat file, about 20mm (0.8in) wide and fairly coarse is perfect for the job. File two slots to relieve cam rotation. The exact spot to file will be located by temporarily installing the cams in the head - even without the bearing caps - and noting where the lobes actually come in contact with the head metal. **Caution!** Restrict filing to the minimum necessary depth, don't overdo it.

By now you should have a great looking cylinder head, even if it is still unfinished. Take one final set of measurements of the intake and exhaust tracts (all at right angles to each other) at all the points shown in the diagram (1/22). Record these values as they may come in handy at some time in the future.

### Valve guides - modification & installation

Sit back now and enjoy the fruit of your careful labors because we will be moving on to a more exacting area, notably the valve guides and especially the valve seats.

New guides, as received, are too long for our modified cylinder head and could stand some reshaping also. In what will follow now, I realize that I am treading the borderline between do-it-yourself and machine shop work. My advice is that both methods should be used. The amount of actual machine shop work required is rock bottom minimal. All that is required of

the machine shop is to shorten the guides and then to taper their noses: this work is done on a lathe. Bring the overall length of the intake guides to 46mm (1.811in), and the exhaust guides to 48mm (1.890in). Next, set the lathe to angle cut, and give a taper to the nose of the guide. The taper will extend about 8-9mm (0.315-0.354in) back from the guide's nose as shown in the diagram (1/24). Make sure that the guide's nose is left with at least 0.5mm (0.020in) wall thickness and not a knife-edge. Intake and exhaust guides are now identical except for length. To set the seal on a job well done, round off any sharp external corners with fine emery cloth.

The guides are now ready to be installed in their respective bores, which in turn means that they (the bores) must be ready to accept them. Clean the guide bores thoroughly by passing rags soaked with cleaning fluid through them a number of times. Make sure these bores are really clean, as even a minute piece of hard dirt may cause a persistent and unexplainable oil leak later on. This happens when the guide, while being hammered into place, drags the little obstacle along the inside of the bore, forming a scratch on the alloy surface. Sometimes this scratch acts as a microscopic oilway to the intake port (that's where it hurts most).

Hammering the guides in requires the use of a special tool which, if not available, can be very easily made on a lathe in about 15 minutes and I mean that - see diagram (1/25). Be extra careful when hammering the guides in. A little silicone spray, like WD-40, sprayed in the guide bores will help some.

The design of the guide installation tool will place the intake guides at their correct height with respect to the follower bore bottoms. The time to

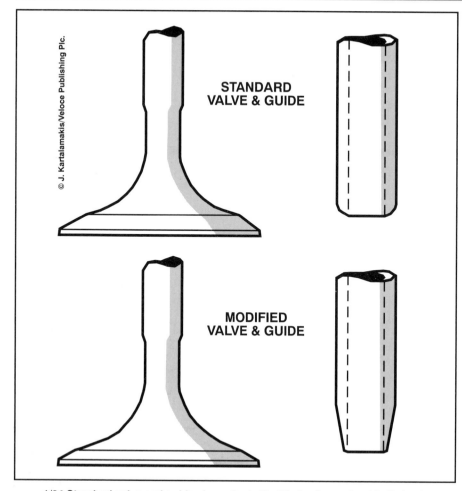

STANDARD
VALVE & GUIDE

MODIFIED
VALVE & GUIDE

© J. Kartalamakis/Veloce Publishing Plc.

**1/24 Standard valve and guide shape (top). Modified valve and guide (below).**

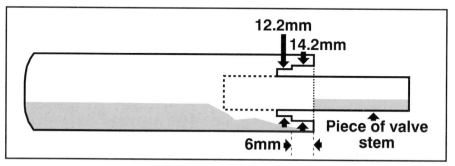

12.2mm

14.2mm

6mm

**Piece of valve stem**

**1/25 Valve guide installation tool detail.**

stop hammering is when the sound changes. This means that the tool has hit bottom (*i.e.* the aluminum head deck). Double-check the protruding height of the intake guides in the cam follower bores. It should be 11.5mm

(0.452in). Turn to the exhaust guides now. **Caution!** Pay attention here, as mistakes are not easily rectified. Do not allow the tool to hit the aluminum deck as you did with the intake guides. After each hammer blow remove the

tool and measure guide protrusion in the cam follower bore. Stop when you have reached 14mm (0.551in). If the whole guide installation business was carried out with care, you will find that a reamer will not be needed to fit the valves properly.

### Valve seats - modification

So, you've got as far as the guides! Very well, your patience is holding up remarkably! Let's move on to the valve seats now. This is a delicate job but, with care, it will be done well in next to no time. This operation can be done on a do-it-yourself basis or by a machine shop. Personally, I feel that this is one of the most critical jobs of the complete modification program and therefore I insist on performing it myself on any head I modify.

You will need two valve seat cutters, preferably new to save time. One will have to be a 47.5 or 50mm diameter for the intake seats, and the other a 42.5mm diameter. I quote these metric sizes because they exist as standard. They must both be of the combination 30 and 45 degree type. The larger seat cutter will have to be put on a lathe and turned down to exactly 45.5mm.

Promise the machinist that it's the last time you'll bother him, as this cutter is very hard and he will probably not like doing it. However, I'm afraid that if you want a perfect job, the cutter will have to be cut to this size.

Well, now that you have your cutters ready and their handle with a 9mm (0.354in) pilot shank, of course, get yourself a Magic Marker (any color will do) or you can use engineer's blue. Start on the intake side and clean, then oil the inside of the guide: everything else being clean too. Mark the whole seat surface with the marker

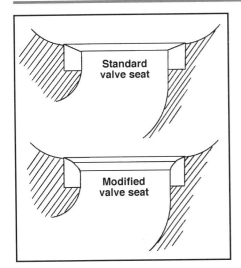

1/26 Top illustration shows standard 30 degree valve seat and lower illustration shows modified dual angle seat of 30 degrees and 45 degrees. The modified seat has much better gas flow properties.

or engineer's blue. You'll have to make the 30 degree cut first. Notice that the cutter happily goes right to the edge of the seat insert, removing even the small lip existing there.

When you are sure that the cutter has squarely contacted the entire seat surface (the Magic Marker or engineer's blue will tell you), stop. Remove the tool and check that the seat formed is not sunk into the aluminum but stands proud of it, however little.

Repeat this process for the remaining three intake seats and clean with a moist rag.

It is time now to make the 45 degree cut inside the 30 degree one just made. **Caution!** Exercise extreme care here as you can very easily ruin the seats with a little too much pressure and persistence. Considerably less effort is required to cut the 45 degree seat so be cautious. Mark the entire 30 degree seat just made with the marker or blue. Insert the tool with the 45 degree cutting surface and cautiously start cutting. After about

two complete turns, remove the tool and very carefully use the vernier calipers to measure the outside diameter of the 45 degree cut just made. It can be spotted easily, as it is the inside diameter of the painted ring (marker paint). Continue cutting very carefully until this diameter becomes exactly 41.6mm (1.637in) and then stop. Repeat this procedure three more times for the other intake seats. This process will leave you with a seat width of about 1.2mm (0.047in), a very good value for road use.

The exhaust valve seat inserts come next. Bid farewell to the intake seat cutting tool; it has served you well. Clean it, oil it and store it someplace safe. Take the small 30 degree cutter and mount it onto the tool shaft. Repeat the seat cutting procedure on the exhaust seats. Start with marking the entire seat with the marker; stop when you have erased (ground) all traces of the marker off the seat.

You now have a proper 30 degree exhaust seat. You must follow this with a 45 degree cut as for the intake, but of different diameter. Upon completing the 30 degree seats and after cleaning them, mark the seat area using the marker. Fit the 45 degree cutter onto the tool shaft and proceed to lightly impress the 45 degree seat inside the existing 30 degree one. **Caution!** Again use care: it is very easy to overdo things and end up with a ruined valve seat. Stop cutting the 45 degree seat, when the inside diameter of the marker paint ring is 36.5mm (1.437in). Repeat this process for the remaining seats, and store the cutter in the same way as previously described for the intake cutter.

All that remains to be done now, as far as the seats are concerned at least, is a little blending with fine emery cloth of the seat into the port. Carefully break the sharp edges left by the cutters until the transition from the

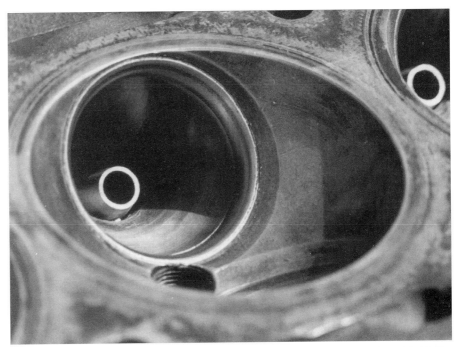

1/27 Oversize seat for 46mm intake valves. Notice rounded seat contours - a great help to flow. These large valves have 45 degree seats, another definite advantage.

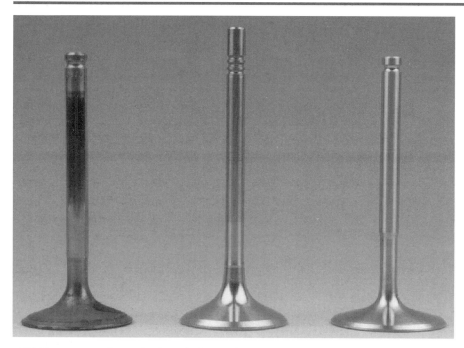

1/28 Three generations of valves. Left, standard 44mm 2000cc item, centre, 44mm Twin Spark valve and, right, oversize 46mm racing valve with a more effective 45 degree seat. Flow improvements were evident with the latter valve with figures approaching those of the GTAm head, which still excelled because of better port entry angle geometry.

port to the actual seat is smooth to the touch.

This is one more time to sit back and admire your work. If you did it conscientiously enough and with an eye for detail, you can figure on about 8 extra horsepower over the standard set-up. More important though than the raw horsepower gain, is the ability to use a wilder camshaft without much loss lower in the rev range. This is brought about by the improved breathing ability of the modified head, especially helped by the enlarged throat area in the intake ports.

### Valves - modification
The time has come now to lap-in (grind-in) the valves. I'm talking here about standard Alfa valves but not of the 1986-on tulip type. Stay away from them because, while they may well be mechanically sturdy, their

shape is very wrong for any kind of performance work and they are heavier too: we can forget about them right here.

As the valves come from the factory (TRW or ATE) they are very good, except for a little lip formed on the inside edge of the actual seat. This lip will have to be ground away and the area smoothed, so that it 'flows' right to the edge of the valve.

Before any of this smoothing work is carried out though, the valves must be lapped onto their respective seats in the cylinder head. This lapping-in procedure is rather straightforward and no tricks are involved here except a minor one, that of determining how wide the seat formed is. Ideal seat width is 0.75-1.1mm (0.030-0.040in) intake and 1.8-2.0mm (0.070-0.080in) exhaust. Seat width can be ascertained with some engineer's blue.

Lightly lap in the first valve until you think you have obtained a narrow, but continuous, seat. Lift the valve, clean the valve and seat, then smear very, I repeat, very little engineer's blue on the seat on the head to form a thin layer all around the seat. Fit the valve into the guide and check - after revolving it a couple of times against the seat - that the blue has transferred onto the valve a continuous unbroken band of color. If any breaks are evident, continue the lapping process. When you have finished, you will observe after cleaning the valve that the actual contact area has dulled a bit - you *are* using new valves, aren't you?

Mark each valve so that you will be able to return it to its respective seat. Take the valves to the machine shop and have the machinist work very carefully on smoothing the lip (just above the seats you have just formed) on the back of each valve. No further work is required on the valves.

The time has come now to clean the head until it is spotless. Use compressed air with a cleaning canister attachment. Fill the canister with proprietary engine cleaning solvent and get it to do the work. Remember you are not only getting rid of dirt, but also dangerous lapping paste (grinding paste) remnants.

### Valve springs - specification and installed height
For a decent power increase from the Alfa 8-valve dohc engine the modern trend is to use valve lifts equal to around 30 per cent of valve head diameter, sometimes even 35 per cent if cam dynamics are appropriate. Of course, the latter doesn't apply to turbo engines as they are force fed. Unfortunately, cams which provide this kind of lift surely over-exert the

stock valve springs. You will definitely have to purchase special springs, suitable for your purpose, such as those offered by Shankle in California or Kent Cams in the UK (the latter with part number VS 28). They are capable of working very hard with high power cams and - this is very important - they do so reliably.

Purchasing a set of high performance valve springs is not all that is required. They must be divided into eight matched sets. By matched I mean that they should have the same tension under the same compression heights. The easiest way to do this is to visit your local engine builder and use his valve spring tester for about twenty minutes. Shuffle around the sixteen inner and outer springs, and try to come up with equal readings under equal heights. To give you a hint, couple the weakest outer spring with the strongest inner one: there's every chance you'll end up with eight well matched sets. If, however, the sets are not exactly matched, use the weakest springs on the intake valves (it's better if the solid intake valves hit the pistons rather than the fragile sodium-filled exhaust valves).

At this point, double-check the two extreme figures supplied by the spring manufacturer, notably tension at the closed valve height, and tension at full lift. Usually makers quote correct figures but, if not, you may have to do a little something about it . . .

First, check the coil bind height. This figure can be checked in a vise, as we are not measuring force, only distance. **Warning!** Take appropriate care, flying valves springs are very dangerous. Record the coil bind height for future reference. It should not be any more than 20.32mm (0.800 in). Next check the tension at a height of 35.56mm (1.4 in), it should be no less than 38.55Kg (85lb) and no more

than 40.82Kg (90lb). Compress the springs to a height of 25.4mm (1in) and check the scale. It should rest somewhere between 83.91 and 88.45Kg (185 and 195lb).

If the springs you have meet the above conditions you are ready to install them on the cylinder head. If they fall outside the above limits get replacements because if you use out of spec springs there are two possible outcomes. If the springs are weaker than our optimum figures, there's a chance that you'll experience valve float or, even worse, a bent valve when the engine is taken to high revs. This condition can also lead to premature camshaft wear, a not very desirable result, I'm sure you'll agree. On the other hand, if your springs are much stronger than desired, two things will surely happen. You'll waste precious engine power to drive the camshafts against the resistance of the strong springs and premature camshaft wear will occur.

We have now come to one of the most important measurements in building an engine, that of measuring and setting installed spring height. (Note: you may prefer to leave checking and adjusting installed height until after head milling if you're going to increase compression ratio - see the relevant section). Sadly, there is no direct way to measure installed height as the spring is not even visible when installed, let alone accessible. You must, therefore, use an indirect technique to achieve your measurement. Here's how you go about it.

Install a valve into its respective guide (remember they were numbered after completing the lapping-in process) and tap it onto its seat a couple of times. Finger pressure is ample. You will need the vernier calipers for this next step. Hold the valve in the closed position securely against the seat, and

measure the height from the follower bore bottom to the top of the valve stem. You can easily do this by placing the flat bottom part of the calipers against the valve stem top, in line with the valve of course, and then extending the caliper rod until it contacts the follower bore base. Record the reading on the caliper. We will call this measurement "A".

Now you must install the valve springs and the rest of the gear, as follows: with the oiled valve in place, drop the spring base around the valve guide and drop a couple of spring washers into it. It is a good idea to use new washers, as old washers are usually badly scored and their 'flat' surfaces are not flat any more. Besides, these items are very inexpensive. Fit the double springs in place and top them off with the spring retainer.

You should know by now that ordinary valve spring compressors don't work on this head, unless you have the necessary special attachment. This goes for the snap action type of valve spring compressor tool too. The standard Alfa type of compressor (Alfa part numbers: A30324 and A30103/10) is of course suitable, if available, and so is the not so common plain C-shaped type of compressor. So much for tool talk.

Use the valve spring compressor now for all it's worth, and fit the valve keepers (split colletts) where they belong. **Warning!** Do this very carefully in light of dire consequences if the unchecked spring and retainer are suddenly released. There are also dire mechanical consequences if a spring comes free under operating conditions. Remove the tool. Now take some sort of flat-nosed punch, and using the hammer, tap the valve stem squarely on its end, while staying out of the line of fire. Not viciously, mind you, but enough to make the valve jump a little. The purpose of this seemingly useless exercise is to help the spring retainer seat itself properly around the keepers.

Now you're in for another measurement using the calipers. Same way as before, butt the caliper end on the end of the valve stem and extend the rod until it contacts the flat part of the top of the spring retainer. Record this measurement and call it "B".

We are ready to produce the much sought after installed height figure by using this simple formula:

*Valve spring installed height - call it "H" - is:*
$H = A-B-4.5$ *in millimetres.*

Let's work out a practical example here to clarify things even more. Suppose measurement "A" is 42mm and measurement "B" is 1.5mm. Using two valve spring washers, we will have an installed height of:

$H = 42-1.5-4.5$
$= 36$ *millimetres*

For our example let's assume that the installed height "H" must be 35mm. In our case, we calculated 36mm. Therefore, we will have to add two more spring washers to take up the one extra millimeter. These washers are each 0.5mm in thickness and very exact at that. In this instance, by using a total of four washers we arrive at the correct installed height. Do not make the mistake of assuming that the same washer set-up will give the same installed height readings for the remaining valves. Variations in follower bore bottom depth and valve seat height due to machining tolerances, or whatever, completely discount this proposition. You have to

repeat the whole process seven more times.

Unless advised otherwise by your spring/cam manufacturer, you should aim to achieve an installed height of between 35-36mm (1.378-1.417in). **Caution!** You must have enough spring travel to accomodate cam lift *and* cover required spring loads, and the spring retainers MUST NOT foul guide oil seals.

## Compression ratio - general & how to increase

The time has come to have the head milled to achieve the desired compression ratio. However, a little pep talk is in order here to ensure a sound decision on how far you can go with *your* car.

When considering the optimum compression ratio we must accept a compromise based on necessity. Problems like the availability of high octane fuel are not easily discounted, especially in North America. Most of Europe still enjoys the availability of premium gas (petrol) with octane ratings of 98 to 101 - though it's likely to become scarcer in the future. In the USA and Canada you'll have to be a little more careful. If you live in an area where only low octane fuel is available, my advice would be to talk to local or national Alfa clubs which should have information on what CR can be used with the fuel available: you might also consider fuel additives. As a rule of thumb, you might find it helpful to know that the CRs of unmodified engines are normally limited to around 10 per cent of fuel RON rating (*eg:* 98 RON fuel = 9.8:1 CR).

If fuel quality were the only factor governing the maximum realistic compression ratio - hereafter called CR - things would be much simpler for

us. However, the biggest factor controlling CR is the type of camshaft to be used. Our project engine, as I said at the start, will put out something like 165 horsepower at about 6200rpm. By quoting this power figure we are automatically constrained to two or three types of available camshaft. Our quest, though, is also for an engine which will have no low speed problems and which will pull strongly and cleanly from 3000rpm on up. Right off the bat I can tell you that we are looking at a 12mm cam or even a 13mm one! You see, lift is torque and higher lifts lower the revs at which maximum power is developed. For the kind of power we are talking about here, we would also have to couple this high lift with a fairly wide duration. We are, in fact, operating in the realm of 290 to 300 degrees of duration. Don't let these numbers scare you away. I will state right here, that an engine so modified with everything done properly, will idle at 800 to 900rpm (no tricks) and it will do so with surprising regularity and smoothness.

You may well ask at this point why have we drifted away from the CR problem? We haven't. The type of cam just described will operate well with a CR of 10.8 to 1 or 11 to one, or, in a more familiar form 10.8:1 or 11:1. This will be satisfactory with fuel of around 96 to 98 octane rating. I must clarify that I am stating the *geometric* CR here. Let's see now why a camshaft may need a different CR to operate efficiently. Why 11:1 instead of 9:1? (To put readers at ease, I will confess to running 13mm cams I designed myself, they are of 290 degrees duration - 260 degrees at 1.27mm (0.050in) of valve lift - and a CR of 11.8:1. I use premium gas of about 96-97 octane and the car performs beautifully from 1500rpm all the way to 7000! This is daily transportation, stop and go, don't forget now.

You are all familiar with the four-stroke engine sequence of events: intake, compression, ignition (expansion), exhaust. You are also familiar with the fact that the intake valve closes some way past the bottom dead center (BDC) point. We will go into why it does so later on, in the appropriate chapter.

You can appreciate the idea that the longer the cam's duration period (the period when the valve is open) is, the later after the beginning of the compression stroke the valve closes. When the valve finally closes, the mixture then trapped inside the cylinder is constrained by the cylinder head, the bore wall and the ascending piston. You can clearly visualize now that as duration gets longer and the valve closes later, the piston is higher up the bore which, therefore, contains less volume of compressible gas than it would with a shorter duration camshaft. Dwell on this point a little, and keep it fresh in your mind.

Let's see now what static CR is. It is simply the geometric ratio of the sum of cylinder displacement volume and combustion chamber volume, divided by the combustion chamber volume. Or, in a simple formula:

$$Static\ CR = \frac{V1+V2}{V2}$$

(V1 = cylinder displacement volume/
V2 = combustion chamber volume)

This formula describes only a static system, not an operating one. If it did describe an operating system, it would only be valid in cases where the intake valve closes at BDC. (And at very low rpm at that, to ensure cylinder filling).

It would be closer to the actual truth if, as far as breathing is concerned, we considered the point at which the intake valve closes to be BDC. In this case, our cylinder would, because of the rising piston, be much smaller (inversely proportional to duration) and we would therefore need a much smaller combustion chamber to come up with a given ratio. And that's exactly what we need to do: decrease the size (volume) of the combustion chamber to raise the CR.

A word of caution concerning engines which have had their CR raised to suit a long duration camshaft is worthwhile here. If, at any time in the future, you decide to fit a milder or stock camshaft in place of the long duration one, you'll be in for a number of problems like overheating, "pinging" ("pinking") and possibly gasket failures. The only easy way around these problems is a thicker than stock head gasket.

Anyway, on the assumption that you are modifying your engine and intend to keep it that way, you should figure on a CR of about 10.8:1 or 11.0:1. Milling the head by an appropriate amount will give you this CR. However, how much to remove from the head will depend on the kind of pistons you are going to use. For example with standard pistons, you'll have to remove in the neighborhood of 1.5 to 1.8mm (0.059-0.070in). With 10.2:1 type pistons you will only need to remove 0.8 to 1mm (0.031-0.039in).

For those of you with a deeper interest in these matters and who demand exactness, I'll explain the long way of determining actual CR and precisely how much metal to remove for required CR later on (after the cylinder block has been assembled). Impatient readers will have to proceed

as outlined below.

## Cylinder head - milling

Take the cylinder head to a machine shop and tell them how much metal to remove. Do not go into shock if they tell you they will have to remove the lower four exhaust studs. It is standard procedure when milling Alfa heads. They are very inexpensive anyway and generally pose no availability problems. At the risk of sounding rude, or even being thrown out of the machine shop, ask them if their flycutter cuts level. This is of extreme importance because, if it doesn't, your engine will forever be blowing head gaskets. A quick check for truth can be made by checking the gasket surface after milling. You should be able to see faint rotation pattern lines in both directions of the cutter travel (or table travel at that).

After milling the head, check its total thickness and compare it with what it was before milling. For the sake of simplicity, I have assumed you are modifying a standard thickness head which is 111.8mm (4.401in) thick.

If the cylinder head you are using has already been milled in the past, you have no choice but to join the serious group of modifiers; you know, those people wielding burettes and calculators.

After milling, use compressed air right there in the machine shop to blow it clean. **Caution!** You need to remove all traces of aluminum chips, especially from oilways and valve guides. Inspect the head very thoroughly for cleanliness before taking it home for assembly.

**Caution!** It's possible with a heavily milled head for the pistons to make contact with the cylinder head. If this problem arises, you'll have to chamfer the pistons or combustion chambers by an appropriate amount.

## Valves & springs - installation

You're now ready to fit the valves and springs. Fit the valve spring bases first, then the intake guide seals. A convenient tool can be made for this small job by using a deep 14mm socket with a suitable extension piece fitted. This 'special' tool will do a good job with standard Alfa seals. For other makes of seal you'll have to improvise your own tool as appropriate. Take it easy when fitting the seals. Notice I didn't say "hammering": very little force is actually needed.

With the guide seals in place, fit the necessary number of washers (as determined when you measured the valve spring installed height). Oil the spotlessly clean working surfaces of valves and guides and proceed to completely assemble the valve and springs. Don't forget to tap the end of the valve stems just lightly enough to make the valves jump onto their seats; I call this insurance.

Your very expensive, in terms of labor mainly, modified cylinder head is complete except for the cams and cam followers, along with their adjusting shims. If necessary, right now is a good time to fit the four new studs on the exhaust side.

Place the entire head assembly in a clean garbage bag for protection and store it safely until the time comes to use it. Now it's time to turn your attention to the cylinder block and, if you want to take a long break, now's the time: you're in for a lot of work.

## CYLINDER BLOCK

While power is actually generated in the cylinder head, it is the components of the cylinder block which transform it to a rotating force and pass it on to the driveline. This process must be performed with the highest possible efficiency: that is, by absorbing as little power as possible itself. What's more, the components of the cylinder block must carry out this task reliably for many millions of revolutions.

As I see it, the cylinder block can be divided into three important parts; the block itself, the rotating and reciprocating assembly and the all important oil pump.

## Cylinder block components - basic preparation

I assume that you have everything disassembled from the cylinder block. If not, now is the time to do it. Give all components a brief cleaning as you will clean them well later on.

As far as the block is concerned, if you find it impossible to remove any or all of the liners after having tried various spot-devised methods, you will need a special tool. Rather than spend time on something that isn't even interesting, you're better off taking the block to your Alfa dealer and let him bang out the liners. This is about the only time you'll need his assistance.

With the liners gone, inspect the inside of the block looking from the top. The tops of the liner holes form a little step with the rest of the water jacket bottom. There must be no pitting evident here or in the cylindrical liner holes.

Take the drill gun, attach a flexible drive line and, to this, attach a 65-75mm (2.5 to 3in) diameter wire brush. You are now equipped to do a great job scrubbing clean the liner bores and abutment faces in the block. Chances are that if you've been using antifreeze instead of just water, pitting will be next to non-existent.

Continue scrubbing with the wire brush until you have got rid of as much of the brown crust on the water jacket as is possible. Do not over-exert yourself here as it is quite difficult to scrub behind the ten studs. Using the wire brush, lightly go over the top area of the block where the head gasket seals. Clean the threads of the studs now as dirt may give you incorrect torque readings later.

Turn the block upside down and brush the bottom gasket surface where the oil pan (sump) mates, and then move to the front of the block to clean the two upright gasket areas which mate with the timing cover. Leave the block aside now, but not before a light cleaning cycle. Compressed air is a lot of help here.

Now shift your attention to the crankshaft and the rods. Operations now described can be handled by a well equipped machine shop, and you will invariably have to pay them a visit anyway. If, however, you think you will derive pleasure from doing everything you can yourself, here's a good way to start.

## Connecting rods - modification

Take the rods to a bench grinder (fitted with a wire brush) and brush them thoroughly all over *except* at the polished thrust surfaces on the big end which must not be touched. Now, using a high speed bench grinder, carefully grind off the forging flash line from the sides of the "I" beam section. Next, use emery paper to very lightly round every corner or sharp edge you see on the rod. Do not touch the area around the bolt head or nut, or the big end bearing surface where flatness is of utmost importance. Continue on with the emery paper to give the rod a semi-polished look all over. To comfort yourself, consider that what you are doing increases fatigue strength by about 2 per cent. I know

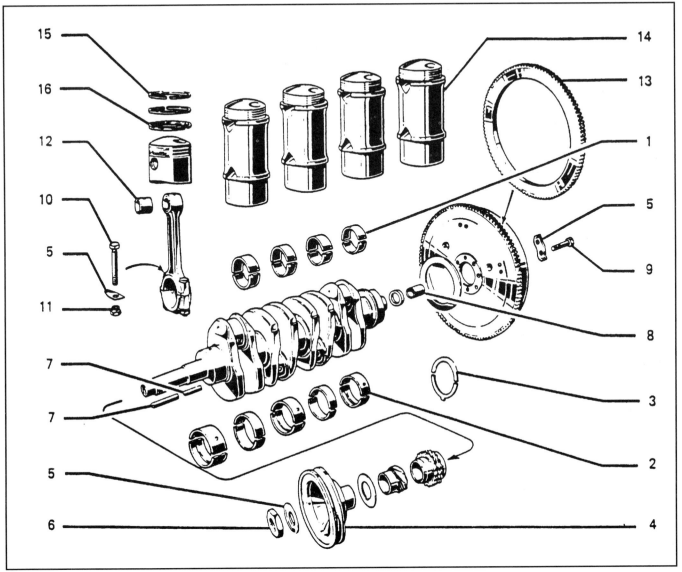

**1/29 Crankshaft, rods, pistons & liners**
1. Connecting rod (big end) bearings 2. Main bearings 3. Thrust washers 4. Crankshaft pulley 5. Lock-tabs (tab washers) 6. Pulley nut 7. Keys 8. Pilot bearing 9. Flywheel bolt 10. Rod bolt 11. Rod nut 12. Connecting rod bushing (small end bearing) 13. Starter ring gear. 14. Piston and liner. 15. Piston rings - compression 16. Piston ring - oil control.

it's not much, but it can also be justified by wanting to do the most professional job possible. Repeat this procedure with the other three rods. Blow or wipe the dirt away and lightly oil them, as you will be surprised at how fast they can rust.

It's worth noting that while the standard rod bolts are very strong and are certainly more than good enough for our 'Project Engine', serious racers should consider modified or special rods which will allow high tensile bolts to thread into the rods themselves and, therefore, do not require the use of nuts.

Well, you're done with the rods or, at least, with your part of the work.

## Crankshaft - cleaning oilways
Now the crankshaft. What Alfa cranks are notorious for, owing to the way oilways are drilled, is gummy deposits in places you cannot see. Drilling out the oilway plugs is necessary if you want to do a thorough job. Start with a 4 or 5mm (0.157-0.197in) drill bit, and you'll have them out in no time.

Now, marvel at the goop that was there all this time and wonder how it got there.

There are six oilway plugs in the Alfa crankshaft, and they have a nasty tendency to come loose, especially on the 2000 engine. I have noticed the same on 1600 and 1800 cranks and feel that it must have some relation to the fact that these cranks are nitrided. Technically, it is beyond me, but oilway plugs do develop kinetic powers on nitrided crankshafts. Such incidents were very rare in the old days of regular crankshafts.

Cleaning the crankshaft oilways is a challenge open to everyone. Personally, I have borrowed my wife's glass cleaner (drinking glasses). You know, the long twisted wire thing with plastic hairs on one end. Really cheap in a supermarket and very handy for oilways. Cut the twisted wire about 200mm (8in) long and use this with the drill gun. Break up the hard deposits with a tough piece of wire and pour a little solvent into the oilway. Insert the improvised oilway cleaner and work back and forth with the drill gun. This is one of the best ways, if not the best, to clean oilways. Work from every possible point of entry pouring in engine cleaning solvent until you are confident there is not a trace of the rubbery substance left.

## Cylinder block components - at the machine shop

Now that you've cleaned the block, cleaned and smoothed the rods and degunked the crankshaft, you're ready to visit your local machine shop and make their day. You'll also need to take along the flywheel and the front pulley (be it early type or vibration damper type). If your car is not an Alfetta, 75 (Milano) or new Giulietta, include the clutch pressure plate. You must also take your new pistons. Leave the liners at home, they're not needed now.

Here's what the machine shop will have to do:

*1) Balance the rods - end to end and total weight.*

*2) Replace the pin-eye (small end) bushing and ream to size, keeping the correct center to center distance.*

*3) Size the big-end journal for proper bearing crush.*

*4) Align-bore the block. This is called peace of mind in other words.*

*5) Machine the crankshaft main and rod journals to achieve the correct clearances you will specify.*

*6) Slim down the flywheel by about 1.36-1.81Kg (3-4lb).*

*7) Balance the crankshaft dynamically by itself first and with pulley and flywheel next. Then, do the same with the clutch pressure plate bolted onto the flywheel.*

*8) Fit the preferred type of bearing shells and adjust end play using correct thrust washers.*

*9) Balance the piston weights.*

## Crankshaft oilway plugs - standard or special?

Try to have all this machine shop work done shortly after payday, as it'll probably put a fair size dent in your pocketbook (wallet). Unfortunately there is no way around it. While still in the machine shop, you have one optional choice to make. I know most of you will say "the hell with it" after you have heard what it's about. After machining the crank and after the oilways have been meticulously blown with compressed air and solvent from all possible directions, oilway plugs will have to be refitted, six of them. Now, here's your choice: do you want to have standard plugs fitted with the inherent chance of their parting company with the crank sometime? Or do you want to do something much more professional and unique? For example you could tap threads into the oilway ends where the plugs go with, say, a 7 x 1mm thread and use suitable Allen-type headless bolts as oil plugs. Note here for the sake of detail that one side of the crank has four holes, the other two: therefore, to retain the crank's well balanced properties, you must use four short bolts and two long (each twice the length of the short ones). This may all sound like a lot of minute detail nonsense, but remember that attention to detail can make the difference between a job well done and a lesser one. Some people like to call their engines "jewels" because of all this detail business. There is no bigger reward than satisfaction that everything in an engine has been considered and all modification work done properly.

If you choose to have the machine shop fit standard oilway plugs, make sure the metal edge around them is hammered so as to distort a little and get in the plugs' way if and when the latter try to escape. This is about all you can do.

However, if perfection and attention to detail is your way, along with a little dose of masochism, you can tap the holes as outlined before. **Caution!** Great care, along with maybe a prayer, is required when tapping the crank as the metal is not only steel but hardened steel at that. If you are still bold enough to try, take pride and heart in the fact that most machinists would refuse this job. Unfortunately care and feeling for things mechanical cannot be taught through a book - you're on your own.

Do not rush things. Use plenty of cutting fluid and work slowly - very slowly. Employ all three types of taps as they come in the box. Figure on about half an hour each hole for the short ones and more than that, about double for the deep ones. When you are finally done (congratulations are due here, seriously) have the crank oilways cleaned out with solvent and compressed air making sure nothing is left wandering around inside. You can fit the small Allen bolts now after having cleaned them and after coating them with Loctite 270 studlock sealant. There you have it, a virtually unique crank. You know that these plugs will never come out, unless you decide for some reason (a possible rebuild) to remove them yourself (which will be easy enough).

## Crankshaft bearing clearances - general

At this point I think I should mention working clearances in the block assembly. Rod and main bearings both should be brought to 0.05mm (0.002 inch). This figure is excellent for all-round use for these engines, and keeps the oil pump happy. Use standard crankshaft thrustwashers and aim for standard endfloat.

There is a chance that your crank will be a bit worn, beyond the point that will give you this clearance figure. If the machine shop can't bring it in with proper sizing and crush of main bearings and rod big ends, the crank will have to be ground to the first undersize. You all calm down now. I know that the 2000 crankshaft supposedly does not have an undersize

instruction, or proper undersize bearings at that, but if you've got this far this won't stop you. You can use the first undersize bearing set from the 1750 engine, with very easy but necessary chamfering of the number four rod bearing shells. 1300,1600 and 1750 engines have no problem with undersize journals. Newer nitrided cranks will have to be nitrided again after resizing.

Here is the correct sequence of events:

The machinist fits the undersize bearing shells (or oversize, depending on which way you look at it) in the block and measures inside diameters after, of course, having torqued everything down properly. He then subtracts 0.05mm (0.002in) (clearance) and comes up with the journal diameter necessary. The same procedure is followed with the rods. The crankshaft is then machined.

If you think that by undersizing the crank, your potential high-revving horsepower goes out the window, cast every fear and doubt out of your mind, as they are completely unfounded in our case. The Alfa crank is extra strong with healthy bearing surfaces. Proper clearances and balancing more than offset any minute amount of metal lost to grinding (and I mean minute compared to the size of the journals).

At this time, you may have a clean crankshaft, but you do not have a clean block yet. Alignment boring has deposited aluminum chips in very strange places, notably inside the holes located in the middle of the main bearing bores. These holes supply oil to the main bearing journals through more holes in numbers 1, 3 and 5 main bearing shells. You can immediately see that they have to be cleaned out, a not very easy proposition. First, you must use a suitably bent wire to

pull out the larger bits of debris which is usually spiral-shaped. Pull out as much as possible at this stage from all three holes. Next use compressed air and a couple of assistants. You will need them to seal with their fingers all other oil holes in the block, so that pressure will be directed entirely at the one hole left open. This should do the job well and good. Blow out all three holes, one at a time, and proceed to clean the block in our usual way, that is, with a strong solvent and, if available, compressed air.

You are ready now to check how close to your specifications regarding bearing clearance the machine shop came. I feel this is a necessary step on assembling any performance engine. The check is done with Plastigage strips. These are very thin threads of waxlike material, which, when compressed, retain their altered shape and produce a well defined picture of how tight they were squeezed. They are supplied conveniently packed in an envelope with a graduated scale printed right on it. It's time now to use this Plastigage.

Stand the block upside down on its ten studs. Again, here I am assuming a spotlessly clean unit.

Take the bearing shells and wipe them clean with a solvent moistened rag. Fit them in their respective seats, observing the locating tabs which fit in matching cut-outs in the block. Carefully lower the (very clean) crankshaft on to the bearings. I hope you haven't left out the thrust bearings. Cut a small length of Plastigage and place it lengthwise on a crank journal and about 6-7mm (0.25in) off center. The length must be such that it reaches almost the whole width of the journal. Now fit a bearing shell inside the corresponding main cap and assemble the cap on the engine block, carefully. Fit the two washers and torque the nuts down alternately, that is, tighten each a little at a time until the required torque is reached. When you have reached 5.3kgfm of torque stop and remove the nuts. Do not rotate the crankshaft at all during this operation. Remove the main bearing cap and observe that the little thread of Plasti-gage has flattened. Place the scale supplied across the strip and see whether it matches up with the speci-fied clearance. If you're lucky it will match up.

Repeat this with a rod journal (big end), but prevent the rod from turning while carrying out the test. One main and one rod journal I believe are enough of a sample to determine clearances. If you feel like checking all the journals please do so. You will be that much surer the job was done well.

### Crankshaft - rear oil seal
Standard oil seals can (and do) get pushed out of position due to high crankcase pressure created by faulty or damaged piston rings. Try to locate a racing-type, metal bound seal (not PVC type) as one of these will seal better and stay in place.

### Crankshaft - installation
The time is right now to start assembling the block. Remove the crankshaft and clean all Plastigage traces from it and from the bearing shells. Remember that all components should be spotlessly clean before reassembly. Oil the bearings and thrustwashers liberally with engine oil as well as the crank itself and lower it in the block for the last time. Oil the main cap bearings, and double-check cleanliness of main cap and block butting surfaces. Lower the main caps on their respective studs and softly tap them until you can feel them mate properly with the block. Do this with all main caps.

Fit the washers and spin the nuts on until they are hard to turn by hand. Take the torque wrench and turn every nut in 1kgfm increments before proceeding to the next one in a sequence which spirals outward from the centre cap. When you have reached 5.3kgfm, stop. Fit the crank pulley/vibration damper temporarily and check that the crank turns freely with no hard spots anywhere. Do this check slowly as you have better feeling this way. If all is well, give the pulley a few spins by hand with snappy mo-tions. The crank should rotate for two complete turns before coming to rest. You can now remove the ten nuts for the last time. Take a moist rag and clean the visible threaded part of the studs. Clean new nuts in solvent and, when dry, apply a little Loctite 270 studlock sealant to the threads. Fit the nuts and slowly torque them to 5.3kgfm as outlined before. If any of the above tests do not work out, chances are you have inserted one or more main bearing caps the wrong way around. If all turned out as expected with the crank, include the machine shop in your Christmas card mailing list!

For the time being, cover the block carefully so that dust won't get to it and then turn your attention to the pistons and rings.

### Piston rings - checking & modification
You could easily skip this next part and go on to the one after it, but dedicated Alfisti are usually perfectionists and love meaningful detail work. (If flattery will get the job done, I'm all for it!)

Using a piston ring tool, very carefully remove the new rings from the new pistons (if they came as-sembled together) trying not to score the relatively soft piston sides. Go

slowly about this as if defusing a landmine. Broken rings are not the prettiest sight, especially when still unused . . .

Check that the ring gaps are large enough by pushing each ring squarely (you can use the piston crown to do this) into a new cylinder liner. Measure the ring gap with feeler gauges and ensure that it meets its (or the piston) manufacturer's ring gap specification - the general rule is 0.102mm (0.004in) of gap per 25.4mm (1in) of bore diameter. Gaps can be increased by carefully, and squarely, filing the ring ends.

Now observe how sharp the ends of the new rings are (even if you didn't have to file them); extremely sharp I should say. Take a very fine grit emery paper and break these sharp corners, just enough so that they don't feel sharp any more. This will alleviate any possibility of scoring the liners - barring a mishap. Exercising the same care as before refit the rings onto the pistons. Observe position and place the rings so that the tiny word "TOP" marked on them is where it suggests it ought to be.

### Pistons - checking clearance
The ringless new pistons should each be slid into the cylinder liner in which they will be used. For each piston/bore measure the clearance between the piston side and the liner bore with feeler gauges.

If you are using forged pistons, be guided by the relevant manufacturer - though optimum clearance is usually 0.356mm (0.0014in) per 25.4mm (1in) of bore size.

As far as normal (cast) pistons are concerned, use the information supplied by the piston manufacturer to establish whether clearance is within tolerance. Note that for a performance engine it is better if clearances are close to the maximum allowed tolerance.

Should piston clearances be out of tolerance, you'll need to check that your new cylinder liners are correctly dimensioned and, if so, take up the problem with the piston manufacturer. It would also be possible to have the liners skimmed in a machine shop to rectify minor clearance problems.

### Pistons, rods and cylinder liners - installation

You are now ready to fit the pistons to the rods - or is it the rods to the pistons? Incidentally, there's advice about piston choice later in this chapter. Before fitting the pistons, check with your shop manual on which way round the rods fit the crank (usually rod number stamp is on exhaust side). With this ascertained, oil the small end bush and fit the piston over the small end. Watch for the correct orientation of the arrow marked on the piston dome. It points towards the exhaust valve. Some aftermarket pistons do not have arrows, but the intake valve relief in the crown is usually larger than the exhaust: if in doubt, check with the piston retailer/manufacturer. It's always advisable to return rods to the bores from which they originally came.

Fit the piston pin (gudgeon pin) - it may help to expand the piston by heating it with a blow lamp - and when it's in, fit each retaining snapring (circlip) in its slot. **Warning!** Take care when fitting snaprings as they have a nasty tendency to fly away at great speed, so protect your eyes at least. **Caution!** Make sure that both snaprings are seated properly, there is no excuse for not doing so. Repeat this procedure with the three other piston and rod assemblies.

Get the cylinder block and stand it the right way up on your work surface, preferably on some wooden blocks. At this time you need to have some rubber lubricant like silicone grease (not sealant). Coat the cylinder liner sealing rings with the rubber grease and apply some to the liner - block mating surfaces - yes, even down the block bores. Drop the liners in place. This should be a very smooth slide provided the block was cleaned as outlined before. When the liners have finally seated properly get ready to fit the piston/rod assemblies. You must use new rod nuts and bolts in the name of reliability; old ones suffer from fatigue, stretch, etc. Fit the bolts into their bores and then, over each protruding bolt shaft, fit a small rubber tube or wrap with masking tape. The reason for doing this is to avoid nicking the crankshaft rod journals with the exposed - and sharp - bolt threads. Oil the piston sides, rings and liner bore. Stagger the ring gaps each by 120 degrees. Carefully fit the assembly in the bore using a piston ring compressor, lightly tapping the top of the piston with a soft hammer and feeling for any point of resistance. The respective crank rod journal should be at its lowest point for this operation.

When the assembly is far enough down the cylinder, turn the block on its side and fit the shell bearings into the rod and corresponding rod cap (making sure the cutouts are correctly positioned). Fit the corresponding rod cap onto the rod bolts after checking that rod and piston are correctly orientated. Thread the rod nuts on finger tight.

Return the block to the upright position. At this point you must fit some means of retaining the liners so that they do not move. The appropriate official Alfa tools (A20117) are very convenient of course but, if these are not available, a number of large sockets and washers slid down the studs and held in place by nuts will work just as well.

Repeat the piston/rod assembly ritual for the remaining bores and turn the block on to its side, not upside down. Remove, from one rod at a time, the nuts and clean them in solvent to remove all traces of oil. Also wipe the bolt threads clean. **Caution!** Look up the rod to make a final check that the bolt heads are properly seated. I say this, as there is every chance that one, or more, rod bolt heads have climbed up and around the rod side: when this happens you will still able to thread the nut on but, if the nut is finally torqued without the bolt being properly seated, the consequence for your engine could be dire.

If all is well, apply Loctite 270 sealant around the bolt threads and fit the nut on quickly using no oil. Tightening a little at a time, alternate between the two nuts until you have torqued them both to 5.5kgfm. Repeat this process with each of the other three rods and that takes care of the reciprocating assembly.

You will have noticed that I haven't mentioned using lockwashers (tab washers) on the rod bolts. Well, I don't use them because they have proved to be troublesome by turning under torquing pressures and by deforming a bit, thus giving erroneous torque readings. Rest assured that the Loctite sealant used is extremely reliable and copes very well with the engine environment, but threads must be truly clean and dry before it is used.

You now have a bolted up block assembly - a "short block" as it is usually called.

### Timing case components - building

Direct your attention to the front of the

block now, the timing case. My recommendation here is to use new upper and lower timing gears. Worn gears that have seen a fair mileage will cause some play, even in a new timing chain. This is especially true if the block has been align-bored. Stand the block up on its back (*i.e.*, with the crankshaft vertical). Fit the bronze washer on top of its related hole (where the large gear nests) and fit the new small (lower) timing chain around the large gear. Now fit the small gear into the new timing chain. This will take some doing, especially with new gears. It may even look like it won't fit but it finally will. Hold both gears as you slide them in their respective mating places after having oiled the bronze bushing. Now slide the oil pump drive gear over the crank (it must be in very good shape without worn teeth, otherwise use a new one). All three gears affect timing accuracy, something essential on any engine especially a modified one.

Fit the front crankshaft seal into its seat, by *gently* and squarely hammering round and round its *closed* face: note that some Vaseline will ease installation. Bring the seal face flush with the aluminum casing and stop there. Place the large washer in front of the oil pump drive gear and prepare to fit the timing cover. Wipe the block/timing cover mating surfaces clean and apply a very thin layer of sealant (gasket cement) such as Permatex form-a-gasket on all four surfaces. Work this sealant into a very thin film with your finger and place the paper gaskets in around the thin studs. **Caution!** Make sure the gasket on the oilway side has the hole cut in the proper place for oil to flow through: don't assume it's correct, as older type gaskets used with cartridge filters have the oil hole in a different place. I have found wrong gaskets in the right box

before, and even boxes with both types of gaskets. Terminal oil starvation is a very undeserving death for a new engine - so take care.

Let the fresh sealant sit for a few minutes before fitting the timing cover. Now slide the cover over the studs and fit the washers and nuts on them. Tighten them firmly but not excessively and in a stepping sequence. When done, use a knife and cut off excess gasket material protruding from both sides of the block, top and bottom. After the sealant has dried sufficiently remove all excess traces of it that have squeezed out of the joints.

You are now ready to turn the block on to its side in order to fit the flywheel, hopefully lightened by about 1.8Kg (4lbs). Use standard procedures here, locking the bolts with Loctite 270 sealant. Observe flywheel/crankshaft alignment: these two components were marked during the dynamic balancing process.

## OIL PUMP

The standard Alfa pump is strong enough for the job, even with

crankshaft bearing clearances increased to 0.088mm (0.0035in) or even 0.10mm (0.004in) provided oil temperatures are well controlled. As a general rule of thumb you'll need 10psi of hot oil pressure for every 1000rpm you intend to use (12psi for really high revvers). High pressure oil filters are available 'off the shelf.'

It's worth modifying the oil pump to render its job easier, to make it more efficient and more reliable but first, no "ifs" or "buts," buy a new pump. Hold the pump body and turn the shaft: it should not bind anywhere as it rotates but this rarely is the case (it will have to be opened up anyway). Try to determine whether there is any axial play (endfloat) on the shaft. If there is, feel its extent and make a mental note of it.

### Oil pump - modification
Remove the four nuts securing the two parts of the pump body together and pull away the lower part. Take a good close look at the free gear. You can see that the two flat surfaces have rough and probably jagged edges where they meet with the helical teeth.

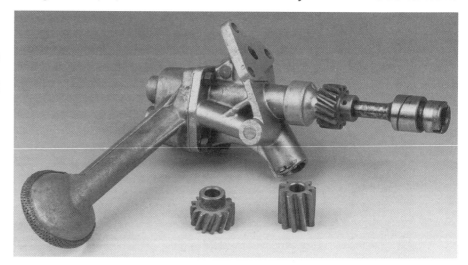

1/30 Typical Alfa oil-pump, this one from an Alfetta engine. 105 type pumps have inclined tooth gears as shown (right), while some 116 pumps have straight cut teeth. Always fit a new pump when building a modified engine.

These rough edges will have to be smoothed out: they scratch the alloy casing little by little, thereby increasing clearance and creating a leakage path for the oil. Use a small nail file to do this job; it doesn't take long to finish it properly. When done with the free gear, do the same with the bottom surface of the fixed gear (you can't work on the top surface without pressing out the gear itself).

You'll have to do something now to minimize axial play or, more precisely, to eliminate it, if possible. Remove the four bottom housing studs. Find a very flat surface (a piece of plate glass is ideal) and lay a piece of 400 or 500 grit emery paper on it. Start sanding the mating surface of the housing cover using firm circular motions. After a little - how little cannot be taught here - when you think you've shaved off a whisker of metal stop sanding and wash all traces of grit and dust off the piece with solvent. Re-insert the studs and fit the housing cover back on the pump body.

Check for endplay. If there's less than there was before you're doing well. It's up to you to consider whether you can decrease it some more. If there is no endplay at all and the shaft can't be turned you've gone too far and you have only yourself to blame. Ideally, there will be no perceptible endplay but the shaft will turn freely without binding: a state which is entirely feasible.

If you have got this far, there is one more pump modification worth its time; that of chamfering the inlet and outlet holes inside the chamber. One is located on the bottom side of the lower housing and the other on the flat lower surface of the upper part. Smooth the sharp corners with an appropriate tool to facilitate oil entry and exit through the pump. Clean out

all metal chips and other waste and make sure nothing has lodged around the pressure relief valve. The only way to do this is to remove the cotter pin, cap, spring and plunger - in that sequence - and blow through with compressed air and/or wash with solvent. After washing all parts of the pump put everything back together. Some adjustment is in order now of the lower housing position to properly seat around the gears. Do not tighten the four bolts tiger tight, but just enough so that you can tap the lower housing around a little. After every tapping rotate the shaft and keep tapping the housing around until the shaft turns with the least restriction, preferably with no restriction at all. At this point tighten the nuts well and double-check for free shaft rotation. What you have now is an excellent blue-printed oil pump; one that will absorb the least power to drive and will put out the highest possible oil quantity. A little work on the pump goes a long way towards ensuring engine longevity and overall high quality of workmanship in your engine.

## Oil pump - installation

The oil pump will now have to be inserted into its housing under the timing cover. Proper pump alignment is not essential, but it is helpful to anyone servicing the engine at a later date. Bring the crankshaft around so that the number 1 piston (the one nearest the timing case) is at TDC, then fit the oil-pump in so that when it seats properly, the distributor drive slot is pointing front to back (as shown in most Alfa repair manuals). Do not omit the little round rubber seal when fitting the pump in the timing cover, as well as liberally oiling the pump outlet to fill, as far as possible, the gear chamber.

Follow proper Alfa procedures, and seal the rear main bearing cap with additional sealant before fitting the actual rear crankshaft seal. This area is notorious for small leaks.

Smear a thin bead of sealant around the bottom gasket surface of the engine and on the gasket surface of the previously well-cleaned oil sump. Wait until the sealant has hardened a bit, fit the gasket and then button up the bottom.

You can bolt the water pump on now (it should be a new one).

## Crankshaft pulley - degreeing & installation

Now to the crankshaft pulley, an item which can be modified so that it is of much help in setting up a modified engine. To perform this additional role it must be graduated in degrees - "degreed" to use the vernacular. It will then permit you to time your camshafts accurately - no matter what type they are - as well as checking the ignition advance curve throughout the rev range.

The pulley can be degreed by placing it in the chuck of a divider head on a milling or engraving machine table. A good machine shop is bound to have one, or the other, or both. You will only ask for marks to be made every two degrees for the sake of clarity. Long marks every 10 degrees, short ones every 2 degrees. Use number punches later to mark out 90 degree intervals. More explicitly you will mark "O" for TDC and BDC, "90" for midpoints in between the two centers and so forth. From the beginning of this operation, do not lose track of the factory TDC line marked with a faint "P" on the pulley. This line will also be your starting point for marking degrees. If you have a knack for detail and the correct size number punches, you can mark digits at 10-

degree intervals: 10, 20, 30, etc, up to 90 and continue back down to 80, 70, 60 and so forth. The reason for dividing the pulley into four 90-degree intervals is that engine events - the four cycles-are referred to as occurring at ATDC, BTDC, ABDC and BBDC (after and before bottom or top dead center).

Having degreed the pulley or not, it's time to fit it on the crankshaft. Before you do this make sure the surface that will come into contact with the seal in the timing cover has been prepared, otherwise the new seal will die young. To prepare the seal area, lap the surface with 500 or 600 grit paper until it is shiny and smooth. Block the flywheel somehow - a long screwdriver wedged against the teeth will do - and bolt the pulley on. Do not use Loctite here as it isn't necessary. Use the factory lockwasher.

Bid farewell to simple matters now as we will get into more meaningful things, the brains of the engine (camshafts and carburetors) and exhaust systems. What we've dealt with so far is, I like to think, the engine's heart and muscles. See how basic biology can explain the workings of an engine? Nature is everywhere!

## CAMSHAFTS

The single most important component in engine modification is the camshaft. It determines where in the rev range the engine will work best and has a great say in how much power can be extracted from the motor. A few years ago there was a general conviction that engines built for high power outputs relatively high up the rev range could not, and were not, relied upon for low speed operation. Barring specialized formula engines, things have changed for the better with much research into the subject of camshafts

having borne a considerable amount of fruit.

### Camshafts - theory

Let's start with some real basics first. What the camshaft does is to open and close the valves, intake and exhaust, in synchronization with required piston/crankshaft position. We can talk of the time that valves are open (which period can also be translated or expressed in degrees of crankshaft rotation) as "duration".

At this point it is necessary to state a fact that has great weight in all this cam talk, a known fact at that. Air has weight and hence it must have inertia. This inertia plays a great part in camshaft design and it is relied upon for proper engine operation.

A little diversion now to the Stone Age of automotive definitions, the four strokes. Induction comes first. Induction means that air and fuel are literally sucked into the cylinder. As the piston descends down the bore it creates a vacuum. If the intake valve is open during this time, air will rush in to fill the void (forget fuel for now). When the piston passes BDC and starts on its way up again, it no longer creates a vacuum, but it is about to push all the freshly drawn-in air back out the intake valve. We avoid this by closing the intake valve. Doing this in light of the ascending piston automatically takes us to the compression stroke. It's that simple! (Well, maybe not quite that simple to purists in thermodynamics, but the description will have to do for our purposes).

Let's take a closer look at what I've just described. The piston is on its way down and reaches BDC. It starts rising again at this point. Air has been piling-in through the open intake valve so far. Enter inertia here, gloriously. There is no way to immediately stop the air column going through the

intake valve when the piston begins to rise, if it is left alone. It will continue to pile into the cylinder for a little while, until the pressure inside the cylinder or, better, lack of vacuum create a "cushion" (or balanced pressure) to eventually stop the in-rushing air. This is really the point at which we want the intake valve to close because we have the most completely filled cylinder that we can get. Had we closed the intake valve earlier, we would have interrupted the flow of the air column, thus losing some charge. On the other hand, had we closed it later, we would have a reversal of flow, air being pushed out of the cylinder by the (remember) still ascending piston.

I sincerely hope that the foregoing does spotlight the most important point in engine timing events: that of intake valve closing. I hope too that I've clearly shown why the intake valve must close some time after BDC if maximum cylinder filling is to be achieved.

Our cam talk becomes very interesting when asking how much after BDC should we close the intake valve? It all depends on inertia. If the air column inertia is high we can close the valve later, ideally just at the point when we have the danger of air flow reversal. If, on the other hand, the air column inertia is low, we'll have to close the valve early after BDC.

Now for the meaty part. Inertia is proportional to speed. High air column inertia occurs at high air speed which, in turn, means that the piston is moving very fast down its bore in the process of creating the vacuum. This, of course, means high rpm when looked at on a continuous process basis.

There you have it! The faster you want your engine to operate, the later you'll have to close the inlet valve to get maximum cylinder charging.

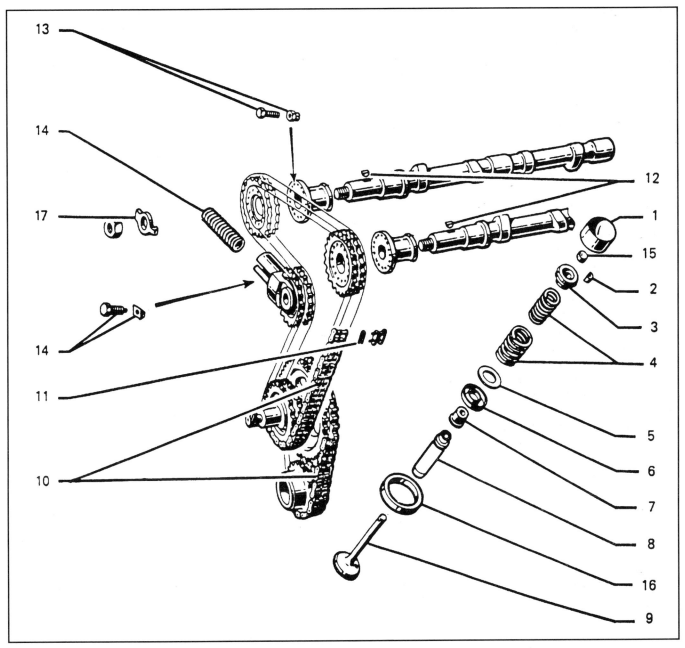

**1/31 Camshaft drive & valve train components**
1. Cam follower 2. Valve keepers (colletts) 3. Spring retainer 4. Valve springs 5. Spring shim 6. Spring base 7. Valve stem oil seal 8. Valve guides 9. Valve 10. Timing chains (upper & lower) 11. Chain master link 12. Sprocket key. 13. Sprocket lock bolt 14. Chain tensioner 15. Valve clearance shim 16. Valve seat insert. 17 Locking washer.

It may seem that I have put events in the wrong order as I will now talk about the opening point of the inlet valve. I believe that, when using all this inertia talk, the inlet closure point can be a good start in getting people to understand how air moves.

Inertia is, again, a major consideration when it comes to inlet valve opening. When the valve opens it does so on the exhaust stroke, at a time when hot exhaust gases are escaping through the open exhaust valve. The outgoing exhaust gases are hot columns of air going down the tubes, literally! They do this at great speed (initially caused by the expansion pressure) but then they suck themselves out of the cylinder, because of the velocity they have developed inside the exhaust tubes. In their rush outward, the exhaust gases create a small vacuum in the cylinder. Think of hot exhaust gas as the crest of a wave moving away. The trailing part of a wave is always a low pressure area. This parallel exactly applies to our exhaust gas scenario.

As there is a vacuum developing inside our cylinder we intend to take advantage of it, by letting it suck air in (forget fuel again). We therefore open the inlet valve, and we do so in the face of the rising piston which is actually chasing after the exhaust gases going out.

Air starts to pile into the cylinder as the exhaust gases keep up the vacuum. By this time, the piston has probably reached TDC and is going past it on its way down the bore. Well, the air coming in has no problem now increasing its speed through the inlet valve. But all this time, the exhaust valve was kept open. Incoming air does not know a cylinder from an exhaust port and it wouldn't mind going out that way. Well, we can't have that. That and something else. With the vacuum developing as a result of the descending piston, we are liable to turn the last of the exhaust gas remnants around and suck them back into the cylinder also. This sounds like a good time to close the exhaust valve, and let only the incoming air fill the cylinder. We have just killed two birds with one stone. You can now see why the inlet valve is open with the piston on its way up and the exhaust valve closed with the piston going down: in fact, both valves open simultaneously for a certain amount of time. This time is called

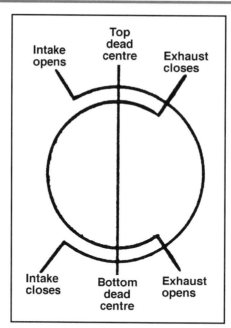

1/32 Typical valve timing diagram showing duration and valve opening and closing points.

"overlap," as the end of the exhaust cycle literally overlaps with the start of the intake cycle (see 1/32 & 1/33).

Back to inertia now. The higher the inertia the outgoing exhaust gas has, the higher the escaping speed that created it. But, higher speed here means a higher vacuum and therefore we can open the inlet valve earlier to

take advantage of it. Also, higher exhaust gas inertia means we can close the exhaust valve later which will help draw more air into the cylinder faster, especially as high inertia means there is less of a chance to turn the outgoing exhaust gases around. As a matter of fact, there is another reason for the late closing of the exhaust valve, that of so-called "supercharging" the cylinder under certain conditions, but that's getting a little too heavy for our present discussion.

We have seen so far that valve timing events can be extended on the sole basis of high rpm. In other words, we can have more beneficial overlap *if* revs are kept high (but remember the word "if" here as things don't always work the way you expect).

Three four stroke events down, one to go: that of exhaust valve opening. Right after detonation (ignition) a great pressure rises in the combustion chamber. This pressure pushes the piston down with great force, we hope, and in turn rotates the crankshaft. By definition, pressure is *Force per unit Area*. Clearly then, as the area gets larger with the bore walls exposed by the descending piston, the original pressure drops and, in fact,

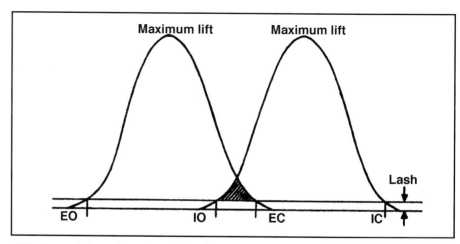

1/33 A more informative valve timing diagram depicting lift as well as duration. Shaded area shows overlap phase.

most of the pressure is spent by the time the piston moves past the mid-point going down. We now have a cylinder full of very hot gases that have already done their chore of pushing the piston. This may be a good time to get rid of them by opening the exhaust valve. As a matter of fact, we could probably use whatever decreasing pressure there is in the cylinder to help push them out! In this case they will escape at great speed, something we have seen used to good purpose in the preceding paragraph. We could, on the other hand, utilize all the pressure left to keep pushing the piston down. But then, when the time came to open the exhaust valve, I'm afraid we'd have to push the spent gases out the door and therefore expend precious energy. It's clearly advantageous to let the exhaust gases help themselves out, especially when their high speed helps out the induction process too.

That takes care of the four events controlling engine breathing. We have seen exactly why duration gets longer, intake and exhaust, as revs rise. This is a key area to understand as it is at the beginning of many long discussions one can have about engine timing.

Another factor greatly affecting performance is the rate at which a valve is opened. This is a bit more difficult to grasp than duration but here it is anyway.

You can have two intake cycles in two different engines with the same duration. However, the two engines have different valve opening characteristics: in engine "A" the valve lifts from its seat very slowly, while in engine "B" the valve snaps open very fast. An example with a few simple numbers may help here. Engines A and B start opening their inlet valves at, say, 40 degrees BTDC. Both at the same time. At the 10 degree BTDC

mark engine A has lifted its valve 2mm (0.08in) and engine B 4mm (0.16in). Total final lift for both engines, or rather their cams, is say, 10mm. You can see here that cam B opens the valve at a faster rate. This very important quantity is actually the acceleration imparted to the valve by the camshaft. Valve acceleration is a deciding factor in camshaft design and must not exceed certain values.

Remember inertia now. To move a stationary object we must do so applying force gradually if we are to avoid impact with it. The same naturally applies to valve gear components. The camshaft must at first contact the valve gently and then begin to push it faster and faster off its seat. The cycle just described is the ramp of the cam followed by the flank. The ramp itself is responsible for a large part of valve train noise.

To continue with the subject of inertia you can see that the heavier an object is, the slower we will have to accelerate it to avoid impact. If we insist on applying great force to accelerate it quickly, we will definitely have to have some kind of "cushion" or balancing counter-force on the other side to keep it from bouncing off. This is one function of the valve springs. The faster we want to accelerate a valve, the heavier the spring must be to keep the valve stem and follower in contact with the camshaft.

All of the problems associated with acceleration apply, with equal vigor, to decelerating the valve gear. The valve must be returned to its seat as gently as it was previously lifted off it. These two particular events have a great effect on camshaft and valve seat life. There is, for the sake of completeness of this discourse, another point to watch for in cam design which also affects camshaft life and that is proper "nose" design. The nose of the cam is

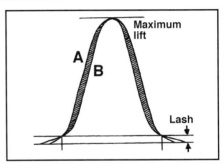

1/34 Cams 'A' and 'B' have the same lift and duration. Shaded area shows actual area difference. Cam 'A' is the higher power unit.

just that, the area beginning a little before and ending a little after the highest lift point (lobe tip). (1/34 & 1/35).

As the valve is being pushed deeper and deeper into the cylinder, there comes a time to turn it around and control its movement until it contacts the seat. Remember now that the valve is moving deeper at a high speed imparted to it by the opening part of the cam. This high speed has endowed the valve with certain inertia. If we are to reverse valve motion at this time we will have to dissipate this inertia. We do this by giving the nose of the cam the needed curvature to slow down the valve, until a point where it is actually stationary for a split second before we reverse its direction of travel. The larger (heavier) the valve

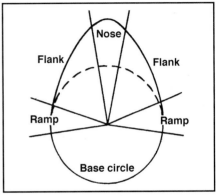

1/35 The camshaft lobe divided into areas.

and its associated components and the faster it moves, the rounder the cam lobe's nose curvature must be and/or the heavier the valve spring. Designers actually strive for a compromise among all these linked variables in order to achieve more power in a wider rpm range with reliability and longevity of the components involved. It is logical then to believe, as I mentioned earlier in this chapter, that yesterday's musclecars can be thought of as ill-mannered beasts compared with those of today, putting out probably more power over a wider rpm range for any given capacity.

Let's leave all this semi-scientific talk and look at how to make practical use of this technology in Alfa dohc engines.

### Camshafts - making your choice

There are many after market high performance cams available for 'our' cars but, on closer inspection, it turns out that there are probably fewer than we'd like to experiment with. You have to remember what we are after here, i.e. an engine with about 160-165 horsepower at about 6200-6300rpm coupled with low-speed tractability (good enough for around town driving) and a regular and even idle (after all, you're probably not the only driver this car has!). For this kind of power we can immediately discount all stock cams, along with some "hot" ones. The *real* problem is we want the power relatively low in the rpm range.

Since we are majoring on the 2000 engine, what we want is lift; in fact, as much of it as we can possibly get without exceeding the stress limits of other mechanical components. Two identical engines having all camshaft characteristics equal except lift, will differ in that the higher lift engine will make more power. The high lift we

want must be combined with a fair amount of duration. However, this duration cannot be higher than a maximum of 310 degrees off the seat if we want any sort of regular idling capability.

We have seen that valves can be opened and closed slowly or quickly for the same duration. This difference can be put down plainly, if we agree to measure duration at an alternative to "off the seat". In the interests of standardization most cam manufacturers have agreed to measure duration at 1.27mm (0.050 inches) off the seat. At this point, the valve has definitely begun to rise and we leave out all misleading degrees introduced by very mild cam ramps. On this basis we can properly compare different camshafts and, after some experience, even predict their behavior in a given engine.

You will find some very informative reading in the pages of the Shankle Automotive Engineering catalog; the pages pertaining to Alfa camshafts. Very few cams have escaped their list, but these are not very well known in Europe either, where companies like Alquati and Colombo Bariani have excelled in the camshaft field.

To summarize, here is what you'll need for your project engine as far as camshaft specifications go (note: data concerns 2000cc engines)

*Lift: 12 to 13mm (0.472in to 0.512in)*

*Duration at 1.27mm (0.050in): 258 to 262 degrees*

*Duration off the seat: 288 to 295 degrees*

Right now is the time to summarize your options. If you carried out

1/36 Author's lobe measuring jig. These lobes start out as trigonometric functions, with some important necessary modifications to cater for ramp design. The resulting coordinates, in polar form, are used in a milling machine with a dividing head to cut the "master" lobes shown. The lobes are checked for accuracy and conformance to the original design in the jig. If all's OK, the lobe is sent to a cam manufacturer who in turn will make the actual camshafts. The author has followed this route a number of times with very good results. The obvious step following cam fabrication is dyno and road testing, to evaluate the soundness of the design.

the recommended modifications you have a well-built engine and a very efficiently breathing cylinder head. You can proceed with the optimized camshaft or you can fit a milder unit. Doing the latter will still give you a strong car with power somewhere over 140 horsepower. This should be enough for most people, especially those driving Spiders and Giulia GT Coupes. These earlier 105-series cars are much lighter than the Alfetta series cars by about 70-140kg (154-308Ib) and, consequently, can be just as fast with less power. Economy will also better with a lesser powered engine. On the subject of economy, let me briefly point out that the engine you have just built with the guidance of this book will use less fuel - even in 140bhp form - than the standard carbureted unit.

The choice of camshaft is yours,

but do remember that none of the modification work you have done so far is invalidated by fitting a milder camshaft. If, on the other hand, you decide to go for the performance specification we originally set out, you must opt for the kind of cam which has the specifics already shown. I tried to have a cam made to the exact specifications shown below -

*Cam lift: 12mm (0.472in)*

*Duration at 1.27mm (0.050in): 265 degrees*

*Duration off the seat: 303 degrees*

What was actually made measured -

*Cam lift: 12mm (0.472in)*

*Duration at 1.27mm (0.050in): 265 degrees*

*Duration off the seat: 303 degrees*

Very good!

The cams were made for me by Kent Cams, a well-known British firm, and are of very good quality steel. They adhered exactly to the desired specification and the results were as expected. Mind you, these are not regrinds; therefore they did not come cheaply! But, then again, quality never does. The Kent Cams part number is JK303. If you decide to use these cams I strongly recommend that you also buy Kent's VS 28 valve springs. Use these without the damper foil. Idle can be set to anything over 700rpm to be smooth and useable and torque is impressive for this type of cam from 3000rpm on up. Very good power is produced after 4500rpm and the car pulls strongly to redline - say, 6800rpm. All this happens with a GTV of 1080kg (2380Ib) plus 75kg (165Ib)

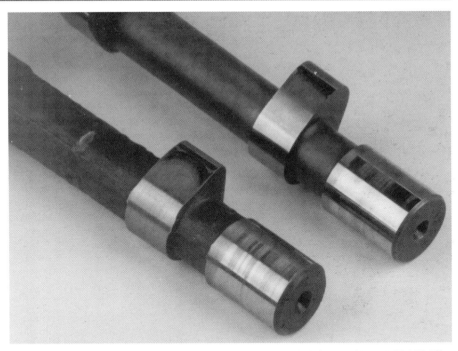

1/37 Notice differences of lobe shape between a standard Alfa cam (105.20.03.200.00) and the excellent quality 12mm lift cam from Kent Cams. The Kent camshaft has run for 30,000 miles in the author's car with no discernible wear whatsoever! These cams are good for 190+ bhp in a well-built 2000 engine with standard valves.

worth of driver. It's really impressive to see a car of this size move about so quickly. If only it weren't for that second gear synchro . . . This particular cam was installed in a 2000 engine having all the mods outlined in this book: Weber 45 DCOEs, 11.8:1 compression ratio, 38mm venturis and a 4 into 1 open exhaust. The resulting 192bhp at 7100rpm, plus excellent pulling power for a heavy car from 3000rpm, are all proof of what can be delivered by an intelligently modified Alfa engine. Encouraged by this first result, I continued research into an even better cam for the 2000cc engine and was finally rewarded. The present 13mm item exhibits excellent low speed properties combined with very good top end power and - yes! - economy. I have not commercialized this design yet as I would like to complete some F3 engine testing first. This cam (remember, 13mm lift) has

performed flawlessly now for over a year in downtown traffic as well as for weekend trips.

1300 and 1600 engines should not need cams with more than 11.5mm (0.452in) lift, and a total of 285-290 degrees off the seat duration. The 1750 (or 1800 in 116 form) could live well enough with cams suggested for the 2000cc motor.

For further camshaft information, if only to trace evolution of the species, I submit to your curiosity a number of cam profile graphs which I have compiled and which appear in the appendices. The coverage of these graphs is by no means complete, nor is any claim made to that end. I am still hunting down any Alfa cam I can find and hopefully, someday, the list will comprise all known Alfa cams filed according to their performance potential. Nevertheless, as it stands now it can give you a pretty good idea of what is available and what you should be looking for, depending on what you want to do with your car. Notice that there is a line calling out the "performance rank" of each cam. To standardize things, I have followed the "performance rank" system used in the Shankle catalog - since it is the only serious Alfa cam listing I could find - and I have aligned my measurements with it: this is what the ranks mean -

adjustment is necessary. I came across this problem a few times and, after giving it some careful thought, came up with a permanent solution. Some of you may scoff at the proposition I am about to make but, since it has so far proven foolproof, I suggest that at least those readers confronting similar problems pay close attention . . .

The problem lies in placing a very thick but exactly sized shim inside the follower and over the valve stem in

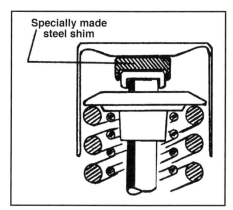

**1/38 Special shim number 1.** Use with reground cams which have undersize lobes. Good for up to 7000rpm in a 2000 engine with special valve springs.

### CAMSHAFT PERFORMANCE RANKS

| Rank | Uses | Best rpm range |
|------|------|----------------|
| 1-4 | General street use | 2000-6000 |
| 5 | Best street | 2500-6500 |
| 7 | Hi-perf. street | 3000-7000 |
| 8 | Hi-perf street/racing | 4000-7200 |
| 9-11 | General racing | 4500-7500 |
| 12-13 | Special hi-rpm racing | - |

"L" = Torque emphasis *Lower* in rpm range.
(See Appendix 2 for graphs)

**1/39 Special shim number 2.** This type can also be used for high rpm engines.

### Valve clearance problems - making special shims

Most cams I have checked are invariably regrinds of a common shaft like the 105020320001 (common and useless one might add) or the 105200320000 (just as useful performance-wise). Naturally, by using regrinds costs are kept low and, if after grinding the hardening process is successful, the resulting cam can be as good as a new one. Life, though, does have its problems, even in this area of things mechanical. There may be a chance, and not a rare chance at all, that after regrinding the lobes are made so small that adjusting valve clearance using the regular shims is impossible as they are not thick enough. True, some firms supply shims 5mm (0.196in) thick which can be ground down to the required size, but this is a tiring process and one that has to be done anew when re-

order to adjust clearance. As a matter of fact, we can use two pieces of metal to take up the required space, one of them being a regular size shim. The other piece can be one of two things: a specially made shim, larger than the stock item it will have to enclose and hold in place, or a ground-down and edge-relieved VW Rabbit (Golf) series adjusting shim. The VW shims (or disks) are 3mm (0.118in) thick at their smallest. They can be used as is with only the outer edge relieved for desperate cases, or they can be ground down by a machine shop to 2mm (0.079in) of thickness and edge relieved which is actually the way I sometimes use them. They weigh barely 12 grams (0.42oz) and this weight poses no undue stresses to the valvegear. Now, I will not recommend this solution to anyone running 8000 or 9000rpm but for a 2000 motor turning at a maximum of 7000rpm this

fix has proved entirely reliable. The accompanying drawings illustrate the alternatives. (1/38 & 1/39).

**Caution!** Do not at this point overlook the importance of excellent follower condition. Wobbling followers, due to large clearances from wear, do destroy camshafts. If the flat surface has any imperfections renew the follower. Do not attempt to lap this surface as it is hardened. If excessive follower bore wear is evident, your easiest recourse is to fit the oversize followers under Alfa part number 101100330803. Unfortunately some machining will be required, so make sure you determine this at an early stage before you assemble the engine.

## PISTONS - THE RIGHT CHOICE & BALANCING

When fitting a high performance camshaft, the first thing to check for is possible valve to piston contact. Fortunately, makers of high compression pistons are well aware of this danger and design their pistons accordingly. They leave valve relief "pockets" or "eyebrows" on the corresponding piston areas directly under the valves. Happily enough, all the high compression Alfa pistons known to the author are so machined and they can be used without fear with all but the most radical racing cams. If you have any doubts, the manufacturer of the performance pistons you want to use will be able to tell you whether they'll work with the cam specification you have in mind. Alternatively, a checking procedure is detailed later.

With your project engine, you can be confident there will be no valve/piston contact problems encountered if you use the (mostly common) Borgo 10.4:1 pistons. These pistons are cast and are therefore not too expensive. You don't really need forged pistons for your engine, unless you plan long hours of circuit racing at high revs.

What about if you want to use standard production pistons? First off, there is no reliability drawback by going to the standard items. As a matter of fact they are better than special pistons in one respect, that of flame travel. You see, the flatter the piston is, the easier it is to ignite and burn the mixture of air and fuel over it. Domed pistons are not advantageous as some may believe, but a drawback to flame propagation: unfortunately they are necessary to obtain higher

1/40 Three generations of competition pistons. Left, Borgo 1600cc piston (circa 1967-1972), center, 2000cc high-dome item: both these pistons are of the slipper variety. Right, Asso 7003 which is a modern, efficient design exemplified by its moderate dome, anti-friction coating, partial skirt and a very light, tapered pin. Piston pins shown are stock and Asso. The author has run Asso pistons for 30,000 miles and they're still in great shape.

1/41 Alfa muscle builders! Asso forged pistons, 46mm valves, 12mm lift cams, special VS28 (Kent Cams) springs and - if you don't have a 'degreed' crankshaft pulley - the absolutely necessary degree wheel.

compression from a given engine. One problem with using stock pistons is the shallow depth of the valve cutouts, preventing the use of anything but a mild cam unless you want to start making compromises in cam/valve timing.

If you really want a top-notch piston at moderate cost, you can opt for the Italian made ASSO type 7003. These are forged, have a reduced friction design, a clean smooth dome with adequate valve reliefs and, as a point of excellence, they are molybdenum coated and have light, tapered pins! You would be hard pressed to find a better piston at the price. Since ASSO do not sell to individuals, you can obtain these pistons from "Gozzoli Autotrasformazioni" in Maranello, Italy, city of the prancing horse rockets! Pistons are also available from manufacturers like Arias Pistons (USA), Cosworth Engineering (UK) and Accralite Pistons (UK) - all make excellent forged pistons for Alfa engines in any size you like.

Unfortunately for the 1300, 1600 and 1750 engines, modern high performance pistons are not readily available 'off the shelf' though the companies mentioned in the previous paragraph could probably make to order. Most owners/modifiers will have to make do with the original Borgo high-performance slipper type pistons or the TI Super variety, assuming they can be located. Alternatively, modifications can be made to standard pistons (deeper valve reliefs, balancing, etc).

Once you have your pistons you should check piston to liner clearance is in accordance with the piston manufacturer's recommendations: generally the upper limit (ie: maximum clearance) is desirable for a high performance engine.

Earlier it was noted that the four new pistons should be equalized in weight (if necessary) at the machine shop. If this work is undertaken, make sure the shop does not remove lots of alloy from inside the piston, thus making it weaker. Instead have the shop taper the inside of the piston pin,

so much easier, and steel's a lot heavier than aluminum!

## VALVE TO PISTON CONTACT - HOW TO CHECK

**Caution!** All these tests must be performed with the cylinder head brought to its final milled thickness. Note that the cam chain should not be fitted.

If you will be satisfied with about 140 or so horsepower, you can use the stock pistons in the 2000 engine. However, with this set up, you must check how much room there is between the valve and the piston with the latter at TDC and the cam in the overlap stage. There is a test for this, but to carry it out you will first have to accurately determine the TDC point on the crankshaft pulley. This procedure applies to all engine types.

Go back to your assembled block and stand it the right way up. Place a wood block or similar object under the rear part of the oil pan to prevent the engine from tilting backward under the weight of the flywheel.

Those of you waiting to accurately measure your engine's CR will return to this test later, after having finished that part of the work: go directly to the appropriate section of the text and come back to this procedure later. The rest of you, with your cylinder heads already milled should drop an old head gasket around the ten studs and then bolt the head on securely. You will now need to borrow a TDC gauge from a friend, your dealer or the club pool. Alternatively, most dial gauges could be mounted to take a reading of piston position. Thread the gauge shaft in the spark plug hole of number 1 cylinder (closest to timing gear) and begin to slowly turn the flywheel clockwise (viewed from the front). When the dial gauge

registers the highest, check to see that the little sheet metal pointer under the water pump points exactly to the "P" mark on the crankshaft pulley or, if the pulley has been degreed, to the zero degree line. If it does not, bend it a little until it does so. Now turn the flywheel until the piston comes to TDC again and repeat the check just to make sure. Some engines have adjustable pointers with a little fixing bolt and you can adjust them by loosening the bolt first.

For those of you with degreed crankshaft pulleys there is one more verification test to be carried out if you really are nuts for precision work. After having completed the above procedure, turn the flywheel in the same direction as before until the gauge drops 2mm (0.08in) as the piston goes down and note the reading in degrees on the pulley. Keep turning the crankshaft until the gauge pointer reads that the piston is 2mm away from the top of its travel on the up stroke and verify that the pulley reads the same number of degrees BTDC as it did ATDC. If it doesn't, you didn't quite set the pointer right on the mark. Adjust the pointer and repeat the procedure until all above checks give correct results.

Now you have a valid and accurate TDC point and can proceed with the valve relief check. Remove the TDC gauge. Rotate the flywheel back from TDC so that the pulley line and the pointer are about 75mm (3in) away from each other. Fit one camshaft in the head first and adjust clearances for its four respective valves. Remove this cam and install the other, repeating the clearance adjustment. The reason for doing one cam at a time is to avoid contact between valves of the same cylinder. The crankshaft is not moved throughout this entire sequence. When all

**1/42 Really useful for any Alfa engine building and maintenance, a box of shims along with a dial gauge. Note that TS engines have 8mm valve stems requiring different shims.**

valve clearances have been adjusted install both cams with the number 1 cylinder lobes facing inward and then line up the cam marks with the cam bearing cap marks.

Time out for a little note here. Try, at all cost, to obtain the front cam bearing caps from a carbureted model 2000 or 1750 engine from 1971 to 1977. Failing this, your next best choice are caps from a 1977 to 1979 2000 fuel-injected engine. The reason for this is that cam timings were changed over the years to provide different engine characteristics. In North America especially, such changes enabled the cars to meet the Environmental Protection Agency (EPA) emission control requirements. Most performance cams happen to use the same basic timing scheme as the carbureted 2000 and 1750 engines, hence the need for cam bearing caps of that origin.

For those of you equipped with degreed pulleys, cam drawings and dial indicators, who also know how to correlate and use all the information, the above paragraph does not apply - but, then again, neither probably does this book!

Back to tech now. You have lined up the cam timing marks. Now, very

slowly turn the crankshaft toward the TDC point. If at any stage resistance to further motion is felt - STOP. A valve has definitely contacted a piston. At this point, you'll have to rethink your cam choice. You'll have to settle for something nearer the stock cam, something like the European Group 1 cam of the early '70s. You should have no problem using such cams, unless your cylinder head was milled a great amount. Keep in mind that even these milder cams can give up to 145bhp (2000 engine) and this power level is not laughable at all. What's more, this kind of power is available under 6000rpm, something that says a lot for flexibility.

If the above interference check turns out well for you, repeat it with all four cylinders in turn. If all is well, there's one more test to do to ascertain that there is at *least* 1.5mm (0.059in) of space between the valve face and the piston crown on overlap: this gap allows for expansion, etc, when the engine is operating.

Bring the crankshaft pulley back to the TDC mark, align the cams with their respective timing marks with the lobes of number 1 cylinder pointing inward. At this point, take the vernier calipers and measure the protrusion of cam followers from their bore castings (numbers 1 and 4 cylinders). Record the measurement. Now turn the cam slowly inwards until the valve is felt to contact the piston. Holding the cam in this position by any convenient means *e.g.* Vise grips (Mole grips), take the same measurement as before. The difference between the two readings is the actual valve-to-piston clearance. If it exceeds the above stated value you can finally breathe a sigh of relief. The more valve to piston clearance you can achieve, the better, otherwise those sodium-filled exhaust valves may hit the pistons, lose their heads

and do very serious damage. To be really thorough, it's worth repeating the test for numbers 2 and 3 cylinders with the crankshaft rotated by half a turn from the TDC position.

If you do need to remove material from the pistons to get the required clearance, a good tip is to grind an old valve so that it has a cutting edge at its head's periphery. Slip the modified valve into the guide, bring the piston to TDC and then put the cylinder head in position on the block (no need to fix it). Push the modified valve down until it contacts the piston (no springs should be fitted) and then spin the valve with your fingers - this will mark the area of the piston to be machined exactly. Do not make the cut-out any larger or deeper than it needs to be.

## COMPRESSION RATIO - MEASURING

For those readers who want to accurately calculate and set their CR (compression ratio), I would recommend the following method of measurement to everyone. There is no excuse to skim on this one if you have done everything else properly.

Here's the way to go about it. The cylinder head must be off and the engine upright, level and secure on your bench or working surface. Bring the number 1 piston (nearest the timing gear) precisely to the TDC mark (which was accurately determined before). Take some grease and seal the gap between the piston and the liner top working it in with your finger. Shift your attention now to the cylinder head. Turn the head upside down and lay it on the cam bearing studs. Take some more grease and work it with your finger around the periphery of both valves. Leave a very thin, yet unbroken, film.

Fit an old head gasket on the

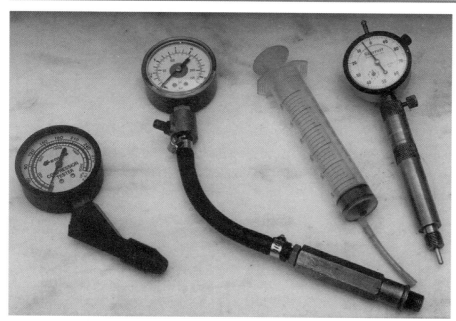

**1/43 Necessary tools for engine building and testing. Two different types of compression gauges are shown, the one on the far left has to be held in place while cranking the engine; the one next to it is of the screw-in type which permits one-man compression tests. The large syringe is used to measure actual combustion chamber volume in cubic centimeters, after TDC is established by the TDC gauge (right).**

block and carefully lower the head down the studs finally torquing it in place. Throughout this process the crankshaft must not be moved at all, not even slightly. Make sure the engine is secure.

You will now need a chemical burette, one of about 100cc (or a 50cc one which will have to be filled twice). Fill the burette with water until exactly on the top mark and carefully bring the spout over the number 1 spark plug hole. Slowly, start filling the combustion chamber with fluid and stop when the level has reached the bottom thread of the spark plug hole. Carefully note the burette reading and record it. Now, if you have any way to siphon the water back out of the chamber, do it. If not, drop the engine on its side and remove the cylinder head. I know this is awkward but no water must be allowed to slip down the liners. It is simpler to use water than paraffin or oil for this test, be-

cause water does not dissolve the grease filling the piston to liner gap. This test is quick and sufficiently accurate for our purpose.

Back to the burette now. The difference between what you filled it up with initially and what is now left in it is the actual combustion chamber volume. It is very easy now to calculate your engine's CR (static or geometric CR) as follows -

$$CR = (322.5+V)/V \ (1300cc)$$
$$CR = (392.5+V)/V \ (1600cc)$$
$$CR = (444.75+V)/V \ (1750cc \ \& \ 1800cc)$$
$$CR = (490.5 + V) /V \ (2000cc)$$

*(V is the difference in cubic centimeters between burette before and after readings: i.e. the combustion chamber volume).*

What you are after for your project engine is a CR of 10.8:1 or

11.0:1 - available fuel grades permitting. Let's settle for 10.8:1, to give ourselves the freedom to reface the cylinder head sometime in the future. For this CR we can calculate the correct combustion chamber volume for, in this example, a 2000 engine -

$$10.8 = 490.5 + V / V$$

$$V = 490.5 / 9.8$$

$$and \ V = 50.05cc$$

Deduct this correct volume from the one you measured and note the difference. This is the amount by which your combustion chamber will have to be reduced in order to obtain the proper volume of 50.05cc. This extra volume represents a certain thickness of cylinder head metal that has to be removed. How much to remove will be calculated in a practical example below:

Suppose your actual combustion chamber measured out to be, say, 60cc. You'll have to decrease this volume to 50.05cc by removing of course 9.95cc of "space." The thickness to machine off the cylinder head in this example is -

$$T = 9.95 / 54.76$$

$$or \ 0.18cm \ (0.046 \ inches)$$

54.76 is the constant used for the 2000 engine. Use constants of 50.26 for the 1750, 47.78 for the 1600, and 43.00 for the 1300.

You should now accurately measure total thickness of the cylinder head so that you can verify the machine shop's work. You do this at two places, one as close to the front as possible and the other near the back. One way to obtain this measurement is to use the vernier calipers as a depth gauge in two of the head mounting holes. Make sure to have clean surfaces on both sides of the head. When you get the head back from the machine shop check that the required amount of metal has been removed and it's a good idea to repeat the volume measurement.

You'll need to check for valve to piston interference as described in the relevant section. Once you've finished, remove the cylinder head.

Note that if during the CR calculation you discover that the CR is too high there are three solutions open to you: 1) obtain another head with more 'meat', 2) have a special, thicker, head gasket made or 3) lower pistons on rods by offset machining of piston pin (small end) bushing (bearing).

## CYLINDER HEAD - INSTALLATION

Clean all block, liner and head mating surfaces and fit a new head gasket onto the block. Now is also the time to drop in - not literally, please - that new upper timing chain. Use any convenient method, it should not present any difficulty. Leave the ends hanging out of the timing cover. Go back to the head and fit the chain tensioner sprocket. This will take some doing. Don't despair if at first you do not succeed. It usually takes a few tries before it can be done right. It will be very helpful if you attach the rectangular lockplate to the tensioner slot with heavy grease before sliding the lot into the bore. This way the lockplate won't fall off and you can install the lockbolt with ease.

One general reminder here. In light of the fact that you are building a quality engine, view everything with a critical eye as far as wear is concerned. Now is the time to renew the camshaft sprockets if they show any signs of

excessive wear.

Another moment to remember has arrived, that of finally installing the cylinder head. Make sure all timing marks are where they should be before proceeding. As far as the new head fixing nuts go, progressively tighten them (working in an outward spiral from the centermost nuts) to 9kgfm of torque - this is a little higher than the factory recommendation. You have a complete engine now, save for the carburetors, air filters and exhaust headers.

## STARTING THE ENGINE AFTER REBUILD

With the engine installed in the car and all fluids properly topped up there are two things to do before turning the key. First, remove the wire feeding the low voltage side of the distributor (so the engine will not start) and second, remove the cam cover and fill the

spaces under the camshafts with engine oil. It's a good idea to use a special camshaft break-in lubricant at this stage too. If none is available mix some heavy gear oil (90W will do) with Molybdenum disulfide and coat the camshaft lobes and followers with it. Refit the camshaft cover and proceed to crank the engine with the starter. Keep your eye on the oil pressure gauge and stop cranking when it registers. At this point reconnect the distributor wire and start the engine. Listen for strange sounds and do not let it idle for the first two minutes or so. Constantly check the gauges while a mechanically experienced attendant is over the engine compartment checking for smoke or leaks of any kind (with a flashlight if necessary).

After a few minutes of running, the engine's ready for initial carburetor adjustment. Settings will have to be a little rich for the first few miles, be-

**1/44 Alfetta GTV engine compartment showing large battery, twin electric fans cooling a special oversize radiator and Weber 45 DCOEs.**

cause of high drag from the new rings. Stop the engine and double check ignition timing settings and engine oil level - don't overfill. Restart the engine and bleed all air out of the cooling system. From this moment on, follow Alfa's factory recommendations on breaking-in the engine and see how difficult this can get sometimes!

There are those who believe that to end up with a really free-revving engine, you must not keep your rpm low during the first few hundred miles. There is no way at all to substantiate this theory, especially when the engine in question has undergone a meticulous level of preparation. True enough, racing engines are broken-in on the dynamometer and very rapidly at that, within a half hour period. These engines, however, are not required to last for thousands of miles, nor do the owners care about extra oil being burned.

# Chapter 2
# FUEL SYSTEM

Throughout the years, Alfa Romeo production cars with four cylinder dohc engines were supplied with three types of carburetor and two types of fuel injection system. Weber, Solex and Dellorto made the carbs, Spica and Bosch were responsible for the fuel injection systems.

By a process of elimination we can determine the easiest of these fuel systems to work with. For a start, stock fuel injection systems are rather complicated for the average do-it-yourselfer and need special instrumentation or facilities to allow testing and modification. Carburetors are more widely diffused among Alfa owners, including defectors from the fuel injection field (particularly the original Spica system). However, things are changing: carbs are getting scarcer and EFI systems have become ultra-reliable, are becoming available as aftermarket systems and are sometimes "tinkerable" in the quest for more power, especially in turbo engines. Tailored fuel injection systems are obviously the way forward for those wishing to modify their engines in countries with more restrictive emissions legislation.

Solex carbs somehow never appealed to hot shoes and were rarely involved in any serious attempt to modify an engine. To date, I have only seen one case where they were retained in a modified car. They worked well enough in that application, but such occasional use will not make them popular. That's all I'm going to say about Solex carbs.

Dellorto carburetors fared a lot better, and have seen their fair share of use in competition vehicles. They seem to work just as well as Weber carbs do and have the same kind of tuneability: the basic difference to Webers being in the acceleration pump circuit. Still, however good Dellorto carbs may be they come nowhere near Webers in popularity, nor in general availability of parts. In this light it is only fair to deal with Webers in the greatest detail possible, short of boring you, that is!

At this point in time, carburetors - Webers in particular - still offer a flexible and relatively inexpensive route to increased power, though their use may mean that you'll fall foul of emissions regulations in some countries/states.

## WEBER CARBURETORS

So far you've built an engine with the utmost of care. Therefore, it's only sensible to completely rebuild the carburetors before bolting them on to your masterpiece. There follows an overhaul procedure which will ensure you have two faultless carburetors. Patience is needed as there are a lot of small bits and pieces involved. If possible, try to have an exploded drawing of the carbs in view when rebuilding them. (2/2).

You'll need two shallow pails or

**2/1 Weber 45 DCOE carburetors. It is essential to properly rebuild DCOE carbs and calibrate them according to your engine's requirements. The most difficult point to calibrate is the transition or progression stage from idle to the main system. Small adjustments in this area may include experimenting with float levels - albeit in very narrow limits around the makers' specifications, say, plus or minus 1mm or so. Carburetor air horns (ram tubes) improve torque (and increase noise) but require different jetting. Long air horns improve low rpm torque. Alfa engines need all the help they can get in this area, as standard intake system length is too short for low and medium rpm. Now you understand why most modern engines have long, snake-like intake runners! Keep in mind that running carbs with open air horns may produce pleasant noises, but engine wear will be increased, especially in dusty areas. You can get mesh covers which will keep out stones.**

**2/2 WEBER 40 & 45 DCOE CARBURETOR COMPONENT PARTS**
1 Jet inspection cover. 2 Top cover hold down screw & lockwasher. 3 Jet cover gasket. 4 Washer. 5 Carburetor top cover. 6 Top cover gasket. 7 Emulsion tube holder. 8 Air corrector jet. 9 Idle jet holder. 10 Emulsion tube. 11 Idle jet. 12 Main jet. 13 Baffle. 14 Choke (40 DCOE). 14A Choke (45 DCOE). 15 Auxiliary venturi (40 DCOE with air horns/ram tubes). 15A Auxiliary venturi (40 DCOE without air horns/ram tubes). 15B Auxiliary venturi (45 DCOE with air horns/ram tubes). 15C Auxiliary venturi (45 DCOE without air horns/ram tubes). 16 Nut. 17 Lockwasher. 18. Air horn tab washer (40 DCOE). 18A Air horn tab washer (45 DCOE). 19 Stud. 20 Ball bearing. 21 Dust cover. 22 Spring. 23 Retaining cover. 24 Throttle lever assembly. 25 Throttle shaft shim washer. 26 Tab washer. 27 Throttle shaft nut. 28 Throttle shaft (40 DCOE). 28A Throttle shaft (45 DCOE). 29 Throttle plate (40 DCOE). 29A Throttle plate (45 DCOE). 30 Throttle plate screw. 31 Locking bolt (45 DCOE). 32 Locking tab (45 DCOE). 33 Fuel bowl bottom cover gasket. 34 Fuel bowl bottom cover. 35 Washer. 36 Fuel bowl bottom cover screw and lockwasher. 37 Accelerator pump control lever. 38 Roll pin. 39 Filter screen. 40 Starter control assembly. 41 Cover plate gasket. 42 Cover plate. 43 Cover plate screw. 44 Washer. 45 Starter control fixing screw. 46. Starter control blanking plate. 47 Blanking plate fixing screw. 48 Throttle lever. 49 Spring. 50 Spring. 51 Idle mixture screw. 52 Throttle stop screw. 53 Accelerator pump piston. 54 Accelerator pump spring. 55 Accelerator pump rod. 56 Accelerator pump spring retaining plate. 57 Starter piston. 58 Starter piston spring. 59 Spring seat. 60 Retaining clip. 61 Progression hole cover. 62 Accelerator pump jet gasket. 63 Pump jet. 64 Accelerator pump jet o-ring. 65 Accelerator pump jet cover screw. 66 Throttle return spring. 67 Throttle return spring anchor plate. 68 Pump bypass jet. 69 Stud. 70 Starter jet. 71 Float (26 gram). 72 Float fulcrum pin. 73 Nedle and seat (spring loaded). 74 Check ball. 75 Weight. 76 Cover screw. 77 Needle and seat gasket. 78 Fuel inlet - dual- 5/16 inch. 79 Fuel inlet bolt. 80 Outer fuel inlet gasket. 81 Fuel inlet - 90 degree - 5/16 inch. 82 Inner fuel inlet gasket. 83 Fuel inlet filter. 84 Fuel inlet filter cover gasket. 85 Fuel inlet cover plug.

pans, one for rough solvent cleaning and the other for rinsing, using the same type of solvent. A large old, but lint free, towel spread out will hold the cleaned parts in order. Cleaning is best accomplished by using a suitable brush with a solvent resistant handle and, say, 25mm (1in) long bristles. Adequate ventilation is a must here as with any operation using solvent. Make sure you have two gasket sets at hand, Weber Part No. 92.0015.05.

### Weber carb - disassembly
Begin by disassembling one carburetor. Start with the winged-nut which holds the jet inspection cover in place. Follow by removing the five cover screws. Remove the cover

carefully so as not to damage the floats hanging from its underside. Push the float pin out and remove the floats. Unscrew the inlet valve and discard it. It will not do for your modified engine as it's too small. You'll need a new one for each carb, size 175 (Weber Part 77401.175).

Remove the inlet filter nut from the top side of the cover and withdraw the filter cup. At the same time remove the inlet fuel unions. All parts must be thrown into the coarse cleaning pan as they are removed.

Take the carb body and remove everything in sight. Be careful not to lose the two little steel balls under two little brass rods under two short brass screws! These will come out by turning

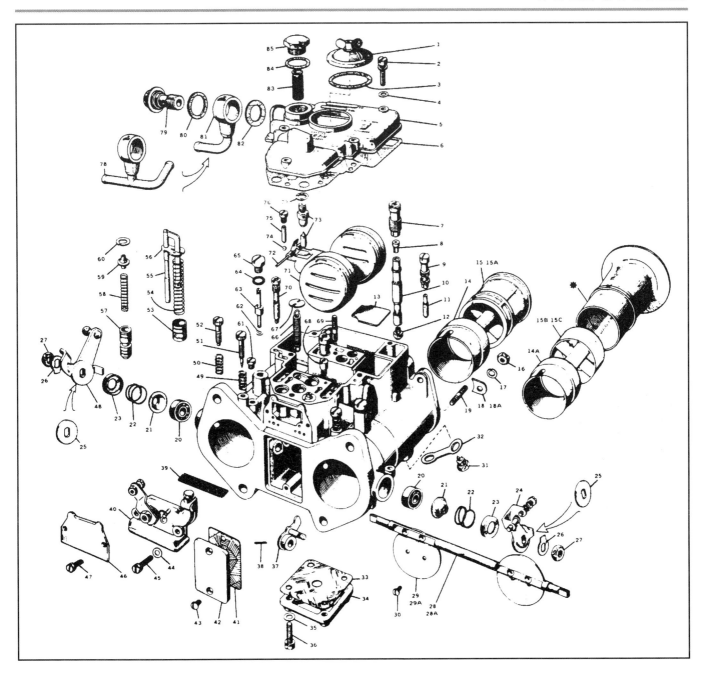

the body upside down after removing the cover screws.

Remove all jets, idle, main, choke and accelerator pump rod and piston. Pry out the two brass pressure rings holding the starter piston springs and remove springs and pistons. These last items will be freed after removing the

starter mechanism held with two screws on the back of the carb body.

Note the pump bypass valve in the bottom of the float chamber and remove it. Turn the body upside down and remove the four bolts holding the bottom cover on. You'll probably find that you have to gently pry the cover

off as it gets stuck most of the time. Remove both idle mixture screws with their springs and washers, the two progression hole cover screws and the two accelerator jet cap screws withdrawing the jets with their soft and tiny seating washers.

You should now have a bare

casting except for the spindles, throttle plates and end seals. Remove the spindle nuts and, if possible, save the lock tabs. Pry out the cover plates from both sides of the shaft. You have now come face to face with a little brass cover/washer. Removing it may sometimes prove difficult as it has a habit of sticking to the alloy housing bore. The proper way to extract these covers is to fit the jaws of thin needle-nosed pliers into the two round holes, and then attempt to rotate the part. Hopefully, this will succeed in breaking it loose, requiring only a gentle pull (while still rotating) to ease it out. If it will not budge, spray a little penetrating oil in the immediate area and take a little rest while the fluid goes to work. The most obstinate cases will have to be handled as you best see fit. **Caution!** Remember that these cover/washers are not available as spare parts and will have to be re-used upon reassembly. They must not, therefore, be distorted beyond reshaping.

With the washers removed save the two springs located inside them and pry out (and discard) the hardened seals. You have now come before the spindle shaft ball bearings. It is not necessary to remove these as they can be cleaned *in situ*.

Turn your attention to the throttle plates (butterflies) now, and first remove the top throttle return spring retainer. Observe now the throttle plate brass screws. These screws are factory peened to prevent their coming loose. Take a flat file and carefully file the peened end of the screws flush with the spindle shaft surface. Having done this, remove the screws using a very snugly fitting screwdriver and by firmly pressing down on them at the same time. True, they are available as spares but there is no need for new screws if you are careful. When you have them all out, observe throttle

plate orientation before sliding them out. Thoroughly clean the bearing area with solvent until it is felt that shaft rotation is completely free of any binding.

One by one, brush all items in the coarse cleaning tray and leave them in the fine clean tray. When all parts have been cleaned turn your attention to the carburetor body. You'll now need a designer's knife or a thin straight blade like those of the retractable type. Note that around the throttle plate and spindle shaft area there is a hard, dark-colored deposit which cannot be removed by solvent brushing alone. Very carefully, so as not to dig into the alloy bore, scrape as much of this deposit away as possible. You'll find it very easy to remove if you allow the blade to follow the round bore contour. When this decarbonizing process is completed thoroughly wash the carb body with solvent, brushing persistently into every crevice and bore. This done, transfer your work to the fine clean tray and, when each part is spotless, place it on the towel to dry. Throttle plates should be scrubbed with non-metallic domestic scouring pads: don't use anything more abrasive.

### Weber carb - rebuild
When all parts are clean and dry, commence the reassembly procedure. Your first major task is to refit and center the throttle plates in their respective bores and to properly pack the spindle bearings with grease. You can use regular automotive grease for this job but, if possible, use a lubricant not soluble in gasoline such as fluorinated grease or a silicone type of agent. Cover the bearing with enough grease to work it through the ball races until it squeezes through to the carburetor bore.

Fit the new seals out of the gasket

set and then the springs followed by those tired looking brass covers. You may have to distort their shape just a bit to keep them in place against the spring tension. The best way to seat them in place is to lightly tap them in, using a socket as a makeshift punch to clear the spindle threads. Tap them in until they're just a hair under the housing lips.

Centering of the spindle shaft must now take priority. To do this you will have to slide the pump rod in place. Look from the back to the middle of the spindle and check whether the pump lever on the shaft squarely contacts the pump rod overhead.

Now fit the spindle end plates and locknuts. Finger tighten the locknuts (over the locktabs) and, using a small wrench, delicately tighten them in place until the endplates are just short of touching the housing and in such a manner that the pump lever/rod relationship is correct. At this time, no sideplay should be felt on the spindle shaft. Bend the locktabs against the nuts.

Slide the throttle plates into their respective slots observing correct orientation. If you are unsure of any positioning of parts, refer to the other still intact carburetor. Hold the spindle in the shut position and insert the four throttle screws. Barely fix them in place until they just nip the plates and prevent their loose wandering. Fit the top end of the throttle return spring onto the little plate and smartly open the throttles about 30 degrees, letting them slam shut each time. This will ensure that they center themselves in the bores. It is of utmost importance that they are free to move not loosely but at the slightest tug of the fingers at this stage. Turn the carburetor around and look into the bores holding it against a light. If properly centered the plates should have a lighted ring around part of their circumference, the same for both. If this is not the case there is a chance of a twisted spindle shaft. To ascertain this, repeat the centering test, one throttle plate at a time, though. When one plate has centered itself tighten its retaining screws a bit and proceed to the other one for a repeat performance. If the light rings are still not the same it's obvious that the area allowing the most light through should be closed a bit. This next step is very easy to perform if proper care is exercised. Get hold of two pairs of pliers and have an assistant hold the throttles wide open. Grip the shaft between the brass screws on both barrels (ONLY the shaft) and suitably twist the spindle as required to return it to its original shape. Don't wonder why the shaft was twisted in the first place, it's a fairly common occurrence, as a matter of fact, brought about by a combination of heavy right foot and improper throttle stop linkage adjustments.

When all is well and the throttle plate centering test is repeated successfully, you must carefully remove the brass screws one at a time, dab the threads of each with Loctite 270 or 601 and finally tighten them in place.

Start fitting all parts into their respective places except the ones which will be changed for calibration purposes. If you are working on 45mm carbs, don't worry about the grubscrew lockwires or locktabs, use Loctite 270 instead. Do not over-tighten these grubscrews; they are meant to hold the venturis in place not deform them.

Repeat the strip and rebuild work on the second carburetor.

## Starter circuit outlet bores - modification

One carburetor modification which assures peace of mind is the sealing of the carbs starter circuit outlet bores. The choke mechanism seems to be a waste of bits and pieces on an Alfa, even in the coldest of climates, owing to the short and straight design of the intake system of the engine. It can therefore be dispensed with, eliminating the possibility of very annoying fuel leaks upsetting proper mixture strength.

If you elect to go the route and seal these passages, you will need a tap of 6 x 1mm size and four short headless Allen type setscrews. Tap the four carburetor body choke outlet bores to a depth of about 12.7mm (0.5in). Dab the setscrews with some Loctite 270 or 601 studlock sealant, and screw them into the now threaded bores so that no part of them is left protruding into the barrel.

## Float levels - setting

Setting the float levels is an easy job if you follow the procedures in appropriate carburetor or repair manuals on Alfa. Generally, levels should range between 7 and 8mm (0.276 and 0.315in) when measured according to instructions - i.e., with the carb cover held vertically and the float tongue just touching (but not depressing) the spring-loaded ball of the needle valve. When the cover is held horizontally and the float hangs down, the distance should be 15mm (0.591in). Float levels have a great effect on performance and economy, so take care in setting them correctly.

## Weber carburetors - what set-up?

Most originally carbureted Alfas will have come equipped with 40mm carbs, except the GTA and TI Super cars. The modified 2000 engine really needs 45mm carbs for power outputs over 145bhp. If you're looking for over 145bhp you must figure on at least 34mm venturis, and if you're going to be taking the engine past 6300rpm you're looking at 36mm. Using larger venturis will make you think the car is faster on the top end, if only because you'll have lost a lot lower down the range. All engines smaller than the 2000 will work very well with 40mm carbs.

To clear things up and help you decide which carb, venturi and jet to use, follow the simple formulae below using the square root function of a calculator -

$$Carb.\ bore\ (mm) = \frac{\sqrt{A \times B}}{40}$$

(A is 490.5 [2000cc], 444.75 [1750cc/1800cc], 392.5 [1600cc], 322.5 [1300cc])
(B is the intended peak horsepower rpm)

Venturi size (mm): use the same formula but divide by 50 instead of 40. Example: a 2000cc engine with peak horsepower at 6500rpm, so -

$$Carb.\ bore = \frac{\sqrt{490.5 \times 6500}}{40} = 44.6mm$$
(45mm in reality)

$$Venturi\ size = \frac{\sqrt{490.5 \times 6500}}{50} = 35.7mm$$
(36mm in reality).

You might like to know that the largest venturi available for the 40DCOE is 36mm, but the set-up is slightly restrictive. If you're going over 34mm in venturi size, you'll get better results from the 45DCOE.

Calibrating the carbs is a job that can be done badly with the greatest of ease. A bad set-up will mean your car

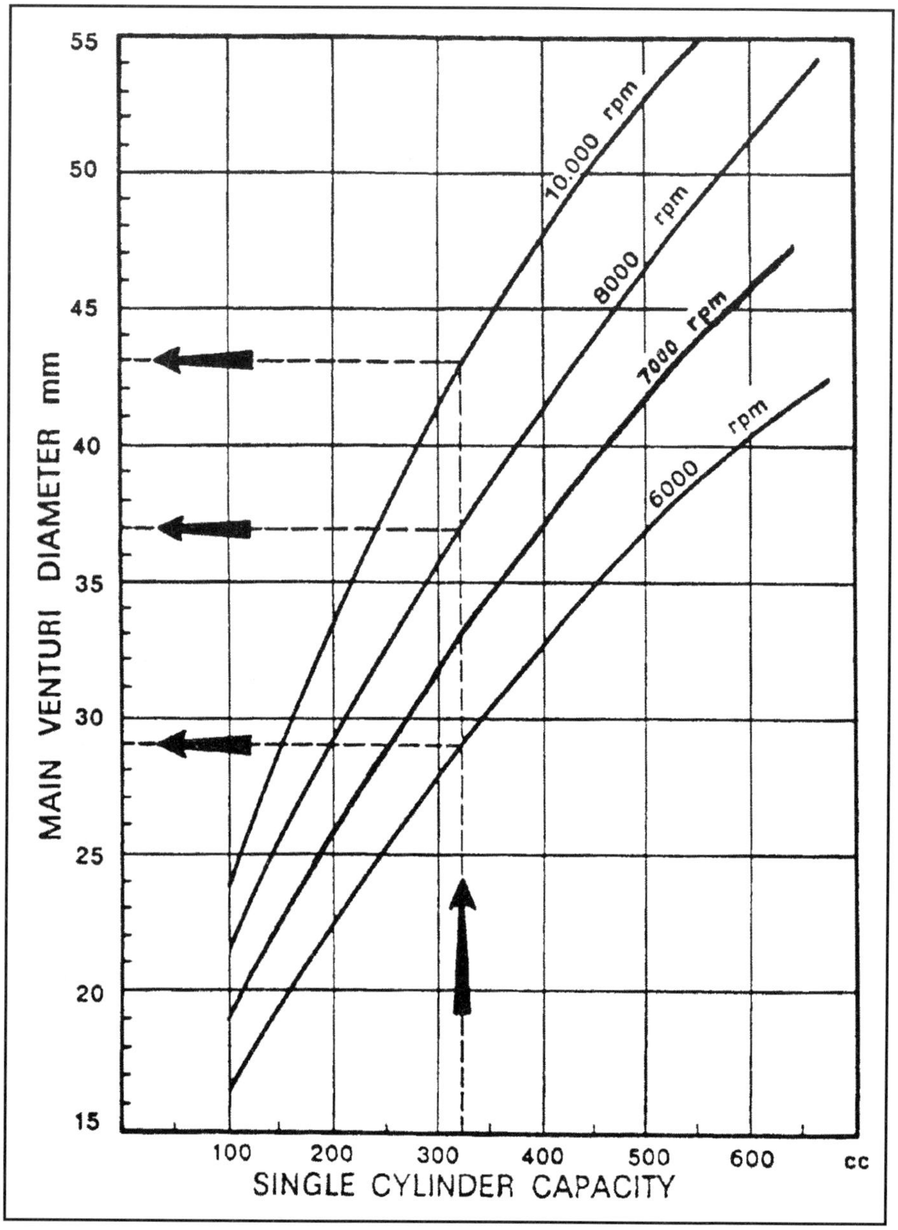


**2/3 Venturi selection diagram. The example for a 1300cc engine (dotted lines and arrows) shows how to use the diagram.**

will be losing power from idle right through to the redline, if it ever gets there in high gear that is.

As a starting point for modified engines of all capacities use a fuel jet of a size arrived at by multiplying the choosen main venturi size by between 3.8 and 4.2 (*eg:* 35mm venturi - 35 x 4 =140 main fuel jet). Optimal air and accelerator jet sizes can only be arrived at by experimentation.

For those of you with 2000 engines and 45mm carbs here are some settings which will definitely put you on the right track. Remember, though, that individual optimal values will be determined by *your* engine's state of tune and road or dyno-testing.

| | |
|---|---|
| *Carburetor:* | *45 DCOE* |
| *Venturi:* | *36mm* |
| *Main jet:* | *150* |
| *Air corrector:* | *175* |
| *Pump jet:* | *40* |
| *Pump stroke:* | *16* |
| *Inlet valve:* | *175* |
| *Pump bypass:* | *45* |
| *Emulsion tube:* | *F16* |
| *Throttle plate angle:* | *79.5 degrees* |

The last line, throttle plate angle, will catch most of you by surprise as you probably never bothered with it. There are carburetors made for small engines and others made for large engines. They could both be 45mm types but try to fit one out of a small engine to a large one and you will see what I mean. Small engines naturally suck less air than large engines, so it makes sense that throttle plates in the idle position will be less open in a small engine (if it's using the same size carb). Because of this, the progression holes will be drilled further to the rear, close enough to the throttle plate to be uncovered by a slight movement off the idle position. If this same carburetor were now installed on a larger engine, it would have to let more air pass at idle. Therefore the throttle plate would have to be cracked open a bit. Damn! Now the first progression hole is uncovered and there is no way to have a decent idle out of the engine. Finally a perfectly sound carburetor is discarded as useless when it was simply meant for another application . . .

To be really truthful, the Weber factory never encouraged any sort of carburetor swapping. It's always us owners left holding the short end of the stick and it's always our fault, too. The moral of all this is that you need to be careful, when fitting alternative carburetors, of problems not so obvious to the untrained eye. Enter here throttle plate angle. If one and the same carburetor body were made available for two cars, one with a small and the other with a large engine, there is bound to be a difference in throttle plate angles (besides calibration variables which you can easily alter). In this case, all you would have to do is obtain the correct angle throttle plates for the larger engine. You see, the higher angle plate would take a longer travel to reach the progression holes than would the lower angle plate.

Notice the absence of any reference so far to the idle jet. Its selection will be entirely and solely dependent upon the type of cam you will be using. Do not assume that a wild cam needs a large idle jet. As it happens, the opposite is true and here's why: long duration cams are not very efficient at low revs, especially so at idle. They are designed to exploit the inertia (remember inertia) of air moving at high speed and cannot as a consequence cater to the very low air speeds encountered at idle. Therefore, to have a correct air/fuel ratio we need a very small idle jet, sometimes smaller than the stock one. For example, in my modified 2000 engine I used a 45F6 idle jet with a full race cam idling at a regular, if unbelievable, 750rpm! Granted, I could not stomp on the accelerator and expect anything to happen, but I believe I made the point as far as idle jets are concerned.

Selection of the idle jet fuel hole will also depend on the cam used and the size of the engine. The "F" code will depend on the engine's progression characteristics and will need some experimenting with.

The best way to optimize carburetor settings is to drive the car through a

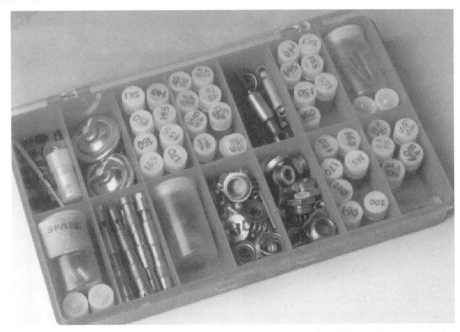

2/4 Expensive, but necessary for proper carb tuning: the jet-box. I have been using this collection for years to tune Webers - it's invaluable!

necessary test sequence with stopwatch in hand; that's if you can't use special instrumentation (more on this later).

I assume you have already taken care of the idle jet by running the car slowly through the progression stage and noting the effects. Correct selection of the idle jet will put matters right up to there. Past that point you have the main jet to contend with until about 4500rpm where weight shifts to the air jet.

Drive the car steadily at 3000rpm on a slightly uphill road and floor the pedal in 4th gear. Hit the stopwatch as you do this. Lift off when you've reached 4500rpm and note how long it took you to get there.

Park somewhere and change one size up in fuel jet. Repeat the test taking the time again. If it took you longer this time you moved the wrong way in jet selection. To double check, repeat the test with a fuel jet one more size up. It should be conclusive now

that going up in size was the wrong move. Repeat the run with a jet one size smaller than the original and if your time improves you're on the right track. If it does not, it could be that the original jet was a lucky guess after all.

Forget about the main jet, and proceed with air jet testing. Repeat the same test as before, only now from 4500rpm to 5500rpm (or even 6000rpm) would be best. Use the same logical reasoning as before to arrive at the jet giving the quickest times.

Needless to say, this dynamometer session (that's exactly what it is) may be highly illegal in many parts of the world: you'll just have to find a venue where it's safe to carry out your tests.

If you can borrow a portable type of fast-reading exhaust gas analyzer (like the Peerless model 600) you can very quickly determine the correct jetting for any application. All you need is a set of jets and a lonely piece

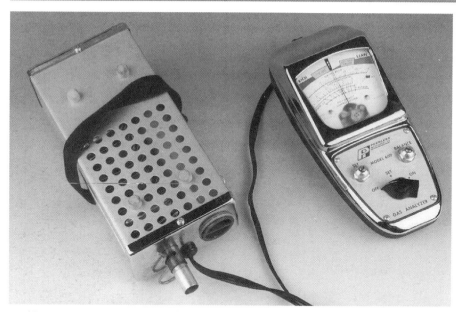

**2/5 Just the instrument for verifying efficient combustion - a fast-reading exhaust analyzer. The sensor on the left is strapped on the rear bumper and the 2-foot probe is inserted into the tailpipe. The reading dial control unit is held by the driver or a passenger, and runs are made at various engine loads and speeds while resulting meter readings are recorded. Lean and rich conditions can quickly be rectified by altering carb jetting or EFI control settings. This way you get maximum power, minimum fuel consumption and a clean exhaust.**

of straight and preferably uphill road. The instrument will show in *every* driving situation (idling, acceleration, part throttle and full power) the mixture strength and you can alter carb calibration to maximize performance and minimize fuel consumption.

Of course, for those with easy access a modern dynamometer and a skilled operator will achieve optimum results fast and accurately. Such operations are also likely to have large selections of jets and venturis to hand.

Last but not least where carbs are concerned check to see that the throttles open the full 90 degrees when the gas pedal hits the floor. No more and no less.

## FUEL PUMP

The standard fuel pump is quite up to the task when confronted with our

project engine. Have the outlet pressure checked and make sure it is

within factory specifications.

If you insist on using electric pumps (ah, those GTA memories clicking away in pairs!) fit a regulator if the pumps are not adjustable and set it to a maximum of 4.5psi.

If your car doesn't have one already, use a fuel filter between the pump and the carbs. The original Fispa or Filter King units are excellent.

## AIRBOX & AIR FILTER

For double Weber cars fitted with the long, cylindrical type of air filter housing (105 from 1968 and 116 series), the stock air filter is fine to use; but the housing it fits in isn't. The problem lies in the central tube which simply does not have enough holes in it. Get hold of a drill gun (electric drill) and attack as many points as you can. You can of course consider fitting this type of filter to earlier or later cars too, though there are a number of aftermarket high-flow filters and filter cases designed to suit twin Weber set-

**2/6 Necessary ingredient of a good Alfa carb set-up is a fuel pressure regulator (left) which must definitely be calibrated with a pressure gauge (right). Electric pumps or not, set the zero-delivery outlet pressure at 4-4.5psi. If your regulator has a glass sight bowl, it's very easy to check for water in the fuel - do it frequently!**

ups. Of course, as far as air boxes go, it would be nice to have a GTA original but, at this time, the proposition is tantamount to dreaming. However, a reasonable replica is available from Romeo Racing in Milan.

Note that when the standard air box is used with 45mm carbs, you need to be sure to enlarge the four holes in the alloy filter box base to a diameter of 49mm (1.929in) so as not to obstruct airflow. Additionally, do not use the standard auxiliary venturis, but opt for the short, thin-wall ones

**2/7 When using 45mm carbs with standard air box, bores must be enlarged and rounded, as shown here, to allow maximum flow.**

certainly bring about a need to change some jet sizes in order to compensate for the altered air flow pattern inside the carburetor bores. You'll find that you'll probably need main jets of one, or even two, sizes larger and possibly an air jet one or two sizes smaller.

**2/8 Long and rare: original 90mm long, angled Weber air horns. They improve low speed torque with suitably calibrated carbs, but they're noisy!**

designed to be used with air horns.

On the subject of air horns (ram pipes), use them if you can, especially the 90mm long ones. When using air horns you must use some kind of stabilizer plate to keep the carbs from vibrating too much, and to anchor the support rod which ties them to the motor mount. Air horns will almost

**2/9 These are theoretically the most efficient type of air horns. Note how the mouths are rounded completely. They are made of spun aluminum. Efficiency is coupled with engine protection when a filter is placed over the horns.**

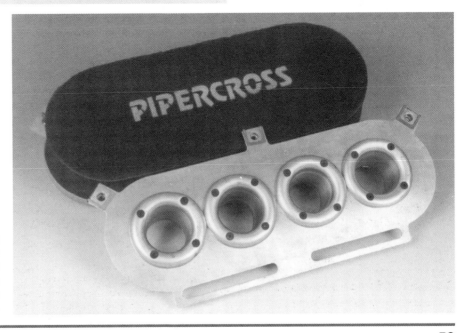

**2/10 Based on a 2.1 litre 4-cylinder engine (not an Alfa), this is a very revealing performance comparison between twin Weber 45 DCOEs and the Weber Alpha EFI system with twin 45 throttle bodies. Impressive power difference is mainly due to lack of venturis in the EFI system, necessary for DCOE low speed operation. EFI system is excellent all-round but relatively expensive. At the time of writing, fitting outlets are few, and you must definitely take your car to them.**

Using air horns will boost mid-range and top end performance with absolutely no detriment to the low end of the scale. Think carefully though about your filtering requirements before moving to air horns. One very good solution is to fit air horns inside specially made filters, like the K&N type for example. These filters let all the air you would like through, while still doing an excellent job of filtering.

## FUEL INJECTION

It's a pity that the Bosch K-jetronic system was never offered on 'our' engine. Of all the injection systems around, it is the simplest one to modify and caters for most any variation in engine parameters. Personally I haven't given up yet on this one. A system out of a BMW 320i or 323i (with two outlets plugged) would do wonders coupled to the Alfa four. It would, of course, have to be used with the Spica manifold with enlarged throttles - no problem there - and an airtight airbox as it utilizes an airflow sensing plate to operate. Time will tell . . . For those looking for an up-to-date engine, and with money to spend, there are excellent electronic fuel injection (EFI) systems already on the market. They are all programmable on a dyno or even

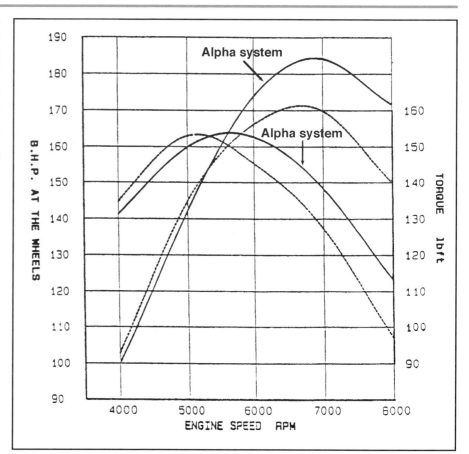

**2/11 Alfa dohc cylinder head with proprietary EFI (electronic fuel injection) throttle bodies, fuel rail and injectors.**

**2/12 Part of a typical EFI system. Clockwise from top left: rising rate fuel pressure regulator, electric fuel pump, the wiring harness and, finally, the brain of the system, the programmable ECU (electronic control unit). Programming is best carried out on a dyno, but some companies offer road-adjustable systems, which require either a special dedicated programmer or a portable PC.**

**2/13 Throttle bodies, fuel rail, injectors and the vital TPS (throttle position sensor) - all of excellent quality and workmanship. These are parts of Haltech's electronic fuel injection system.**

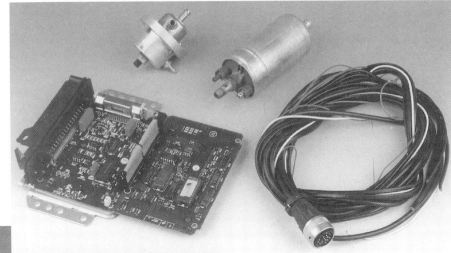

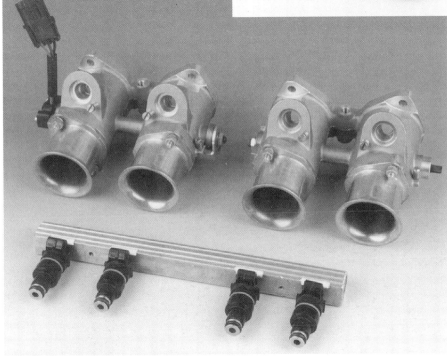

while driving the car and can smooth out tractability problems in highly modified engines. Weber Alpha, Lumenition, Zytek, Motec, Haltech and others offer PC programmable systems. Lumenition and Motec offer hand-held programmers. These systems come complete (or less if you want) with throttle bodies, fuel pumps, wiring looms, and of course the ECU (Electronic Control Unit). They can even be installed in most cases in catalyst equipped cars. The only real-time driver adjustable EFI so far is the set-up offered by Microdynamics in the U.K. I consider it to be the most easy to use system, though not nearly as sophisticated as any of the others.

For cars equipped with factory EFI systems, the well-known "chip changing" is the best solution for a modified engine, provided you find a reputable expert. You can expect between 7 and 10bhp for the 2000 engine in unmodified form, and a bit less of course for the injected 1600 and 1800. Be aware that while performance will improve, gas mileage will

**2/14 Mounting surfaces of aftermarket EFI system throttle bodies (Haltech in this case), duplicates carburetor mounting and bolts directly to mounting blocks.**

2/15 Weber-Alpha EFI system. Very sophisticated and effective, but only a handful of authorized dealers are equipped to carry out this conversion.

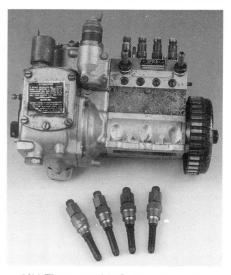

2/16 The venerable Spica mechanical pump and injectors. This precision-made masterpiece has its origins in the famous 33 TT3 cars and the Montreal. Unfortunately this unit cannot be recalibrated by mere mortals, requiring purpose-made innards, the design and construction of which are only possible in factory level workshops and development labs. Features of this system are timed injection capability (for each cylinder), plus excellent fuel atomization due to the system's high operating pressure (about 500psi)

decrease (you never get something for nothing), and for those of you who care, the catalyst will not last as long as it otherwise would.

For non-catalyst EFI cars, I have developed a little electronic circuit, which changes the air/fuel ratio for higher power upon demand from the driver. It adds about 7bhp during acceleration, for instance when passing other cars on the road.

A few words now for the SPICA injected 1750 and 2000 engines of North American habitat. Despite the fact that the Spica FI pumps are mechanical jewels - much better than the Bosch equivalent - they do not lend themselves readily to modifications. The one essential modification, would entail replacement of the "heart" of the system, the barrel-shaped cam which controls fuel delivery to the engine. This 3-dimensional cam cannot be modified, and any replacement used must be specifically designed for the particular engine. Work of this kind is only possible in engine development centers - well outside of our capabilities, to say the least! I'm afraid that the only recourse open to owners of SPICA equipped cars is the installation of dual carbs, or aftermarket specialized EFI systems.

# Chapter 3
# IGNITION AND ELECTRICS

Most people have the idea that all you have to do to the ignition system of a car when modifying it is to add a high quality aftermarket electronic ignition. While this in itself is a valid and, in most instances, necessary step, it is by no means the only one required to cater for a modified powerplant.

## DISTRIBUTOR

The distributor is the most important component in the chain of electrically related items in the ignition system. It has the task of supplying a spark at the correct time for proper ignition.

As revs rise, the spark must occur earlier and earlier in the compression cycle to allow for flame propagation speed. The device which "moves" the spark around is the advance mechanism of the distributor. This mechanism incorporates two springs and two weights, sometimes called governor weights, which move outward, centrifugally, against the resistance of their tension springs. When the weights move out (or in), they rotate the contact breaker cam away from its regular rest position in the process. The ark of this rotation gets longer with rising revs as centrifugal force throws the weights farther out against the springs. From a tuner's point of view, we are very interested in the way this spring/weight relationship works. This relationship was determined at the factory a long time ago for the standard engine.

It should be noted that the distributor spindle which carries the breaker cam and rotor arm rotates at half the crankshaft speed, which is all it needs to do to cover the whole four stroke cycle in one of its revolutions.

A little deviation is in order here to discuss a few basics. Spark advance requirements are very closely related to combustion chamber size and design, CR, mixture strength, temperature, volumetric efficiency and, of course, rpm. Right away, you'll see that in seriously modifying an engine like you have, most of these values are altered. As a matter of fact, the only one that hasn't changed is the design of the combustion chamber.

The need for a different spark advance curve (hereafter just called "curve" for short) for our project engine is evident. We must proceed to consider how it must be changed in light of the altered values. We will take these quantities one at a time and note their effect on advance needs -

*a) Smaller combustion chamber means a higher CR and this in turn means that the flame front has a more compact area to cover than before. Consequently, less ignition advance is needed.*

*b) A lean mixture burns faster than a rich one, requiring less advance.*

*c) Low volumetric efficiency systems need more spark advance for complete combustion.*

*d) As revs rise spark advance gets longer, all other things being equal.*

It would be impossible for anyone without special knowledge and special instrumentation to consider the effect of combining all these variables and come up with an ideal advance curve. Even then, the resulting curve would have to be tried out on the dynamometer to verify its correct shape.

The foregoing was only meant to impress upon you the importance of the curve and to understand the many considerations required in its optimization. Fortunately, when it comes to practically modifying a curve, life is much simpler than you might expect. Throughout the years, different modifiers have tackled the problem and, not surprisingly, they all came up with much the same curve for increased performance.

For those of you who would prefer to buy a distributor with the new curve built into it there are specialists and manufacturers like Aldon or Microdynamics who can supply what you need. For those who insist on modifying even this part of the engine themselves, I will outline a course of action.

### Distributor - advance curve modification

First, you must have in hand a known good distributor, Bosch part number 0 231 178 006. By saying "good" I mean one with no sideplay at all on the distributor spindle. Do not take this requirement lightly, because if there is sideplay, your spark timing will vary excessively (spark scatter). It is a good idea at this time to check and see how this stock distributor performs in your engine. There is a chance that it works perfectly (this often happens if you have a fairly high CR and lower than about 96 octane fuel). If, however,

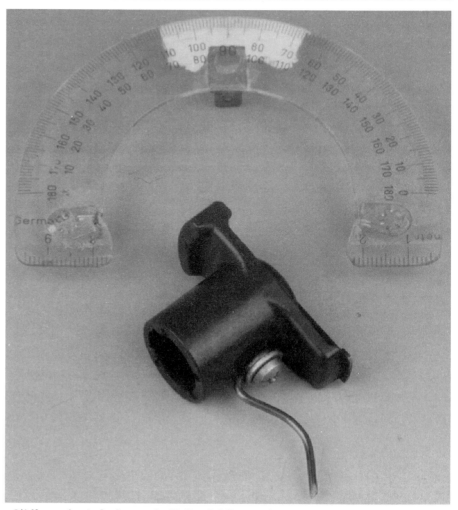

3/1 If you plan to fool around with the distributor advance curve, the items shown are necessary. Plastic protractors (top) are cheap and easy to find, and the modified rotor with the wire pointer you can easily make up. You'll have to carefully tap a thread in the rotor body to mount the machine screw as illustrated.

your CR is low and your cams on the wild side you will have to modify the advance mechanism as follows.

You'll need a plastic protractor; a cheap one will do. Find an old rotor and, by any suitable method, mount a sideways pointing wire pointer - about 50mm (2in) long - on it. (3/1).

You'll now need something that isn't very common, the primary spring from a Bosch distributor as fitted to a Volkswagen Golf (the European version of the Rabbit). You shouldn't have too much trouble ordering one at

a VW dealership. Don't get me wrong here. The spring does not strictly have to come from a VW: it's just that I've found that this particular item works very well in our intended application. Any spring with comparable characteristics will do.

Remove the points and condenser, then the two outside screws holding the cap clips and the breaker plate. Grip the breaker plate with a pair of long-nose pliers and, by suitably tilting and rotating, lift it off.

You are now confronted with the

advance mechanism, the springs and the weights. You'll notice that while the two weights are identical the springs are not. One spring is short and the other is longer end to end, incorporating a long loop on the end closer to the center. You can see that the short spring is already under tension. This is the primary spring. The longer spring comes into effect when it is also put under tension. This happens when it is moved to the point where the long loop contacts the plastic covered post inside it. It is obvious that up to a point of plate rotation only the primary spring resists motion. After this, the secondary spring enters the picture and the sum of two springs counters further plate rotation. The plate, of course, is rotated by the centrifugal action of the weights. What we want to do is to substitute a weaker primary spring in place of the existing one, and then ensure that the secondary spring comes into effect when we want it to.

So, you've found a weaker spring somewhere; that's very good. Remove the old primary spring first. Do not fit the new spring in just yet. Grip the bottom drive gear in a vise and get hold of the protractor and the rotor with the pointer on it. Find some way to fix the protractor on the top lip of the housing so that it is concentric with the shaft. Block any movement of the housing relative to the shaft. The only movable thing now should be the advance mechanism. Fit the special rotor you made and bring the wire pointer to zero degrees on the protractor with the mechanism fully counterclockwise. Take a long thin screwdriver and very carefully push out one of the weights in the mechanism causing the rotor to rotate clockwise. You will get to a point where resistance to free motion is felt as the secondary spring comes into effect. Note the protractor reading at this point. Repeat this test carefully several times to make sure you have repeat-

ability of the results in degrees.

Most probably the reading in degrees will be 6 or 7. We want to make this 10 or 11. You must carefully, but firmly, bend the outer tab holding the secondary spring inwards and then repeat the simple test. Keep at it until the protractor reads 10 degrees. Remove the protractor and the false rotor and fit the new primary spring inside.

Return the breaker plate into its housing and secure it and the spring clips with the two screws. Fit new points and condenser, oil (very sparingly) the shaft center, top it all off with a new rotor and distributor cap and there you have it. A modified distributor which has cost you next to nothing in parts and, more importantly, made by you.

What you have done is to raise the lower part of the curve to compensate for lost volumetric efficiency because of using a wild cam. To appreciate what you have achieved, an A to B comparison would be very enlightening. Drive the modified car with the converted distributor and observe engine behavior, especially when accelerating from lower rpm. Repeat the test with a standard distributor and note the difference.

If you like stomping on the gaspedal of an engine with a high CR and pre-ignition (detonation) is a problem, try using the Bosch 0.231.110.006 distributor in stock form or, if needed, with reduced primary curve - say 3 or 4 degrees (which will reduce preignition under acceleration).

As a last point on this topic, note that, after about 1980, all Alfa Romeo distributors had no contact breaker points. Distributor advance curve modification is just as valid for these distributors, the only difference being the disassembly and assembly process due to different parts used. These

**3/2 This is the way the two simple 'special' tools are installed. After you ascertain the advance curve break points, verify the complete curve on a distributor testing machine.**

distributors must be used with their original ignition "box," unless you are very adept (and equipped) electronics-wise.

## IGNITION SYSTEM - GENERAL

Besides requiring a revised advance curve, a modified engine places increased demands on the High Voltage (Tension) System. It is not enough just to fit a high-performance ignition coil, especially when some so-named coils are inferior to the standard factory item! A good electronic ignition system is a necessity as are a good high-output coil, good high voltage wires (HT leads) and spark plugs of the correct heat range and shape. While I cannot recommend any electronic ignition units specifically, it would be a good idea to stick to what racers use. Mind you, electronic ignition systems don't come cheaply, but are powerful.

### Ignition - timing

It's difficult to be specific here because the ideal ignition timing for *your* car's engine can only be found by experimentation. As a guide, high performance Alfa engines are usually happiest with static ignition timing set somewhere between 3 and 10 degrees BTDC. The aim is to achieve maximum performance and throttle response without pre-ignition (pinging/pinking).

### Ignition coil, spark plugs - choosing

As far as coils go I can recommend the Marelli BK3A or Bosch supercoil (red in color) for one. Use good quality wire-core high voltage wires. 2 (kilohms) of resistance is adequate for radio noise suppression. I use Champion N2C or NGK B9ES plugs

3/3 A powerful engine requires a powerful spark. Use a good, proprietary, high-power electronic ignition system, a good high-power coil (in this case the Marelli BK3A) and suitable spark plugs (in this case NGK B10ES racing plugs). Use wire core cables with silicone rubber boots. Don't look for this CD (capacitive discharge) unit in the shops, it was designed and built by the author. The unit delivers 210 millijoules of spark energy and it is triggered by a modified Bosch inductive distributor. Racing plugs do not foul with this set-up, even in downtown traffic jams!

in my car. For wilder engines use NGK B10ES or expensive Champion N84G for racing. Static advance should be somewhere between 2 and 4 degrees BTDC. Driving style and vehicle use will finally determine the correct plug to use. The above recommended plugs are not meant for stop and go traffic. The N3G is more suitable for city driving than the other two.

### Electronic ignition systems - choosing

I won't make any recommendation regarding whether to use a capacitive or inductive discharge type of electronic ignition because recent advances in technology have helped develop excellent examples of both types: the choice is yours. If you opt for an expensive electronic fuel injection system (see relevant chapter) chances are you will receive - as an integral part of the system - a

programmable ignition system. Programming is best done on the rolling road or engine dynamometer. Advanced systems even have knock sensors for ultimate spark control. With this kind of system you really can have a state-of-the-art engine! (At a state-of-the-art price, of course!)

### Tachometer (rev-counter) - accuracy

While not a part of the ignition system, the tachometer is the second most important instrument in your car. Unfortunately very few units are accurate, and some are so far off that they are potentially dangerous to your engine's health.

While I'm afraid it isn't easy to correct an inaccurate electronic tachometer without getting into the circuit itself, checking one out for accuracy is not difficult for any half-decent electronics expert. If you have a friend capable of doing this, it's well worth taking him or her out to lunch sometime. People like me are nuts for accuracy: I went through two factory tachometers in my GTV before I gave up. I then proceeded to build my own circuit for one, couple it with a very accurate mechanical meter movement, test it thoroughly and finally install it in place of the original. For the record, the first Veglia unit showed 2200rpm for a true 2000 and 5700rpm for a true 6000. The second one was almost correct up to 3000rpm but then took off and read 6200rpm for a true 6000!

Mechanical tachs are a bit more difficult to work on. But, if you do get the hang of it, they can be corrected by magnetizing or demagnetizing the driven plate inside. As a rule they are more accurate than their electronic counterparts.

## GENERATOR, STARTER MOTOR & BATTERY

### Generator

If your car came originally with a generator replace it with a good high current alternator. 55amp types and over are very good, and they have built-in regulators as a bonus feature. There is really nothing more to say about alternators except watch out for excessive belt tension, a condition leading to premature water pump failure and alternator bearing problems.

### Starter motor

As far as starter motors go, opt for the latest models (like the Alfa 75 cars) incorporating internal reducer gear drives. These starters are lighter and much more powerful than older ones. They are made by both Bosch and Ducellier.

### Battery

Unless you are going racing (when battery type is often determined by regulations), install the biggest, most powerful battery you can find! High compression engines need a lot of torque to rotate comfortably, especially in freezing weather.

# Chapter 4
# EXHAUST SYSTEM

We have arrived at the part of the engine where there is not much for the do-it-yourself owner to do, other than specify what is wanted to someone who has the facilities to make it.

The exhaust system must not be thought of as a separate item: it is a part of the entire breathing system of the engine. There exists much interaction between the exhaust and the intake system, and changes in camshaft timing should ideally be complimented by exhaust system changes. You can ensure that the exhaust system's physical dimensions are such, that it operates efficiently in the rev range mostly used. Do this by designing the system according to some rules, many of which are empirical.

## Exhaust system - should you use the standard set-up?

As in most production exhaust systems, Alfa's standard exhausts are plagued with undersize tubing. Small diameter pipes do not permit rapid evacuation of exhaust gases and thereby act as a 'cork' to the gas flow of higher rpm horsepower. Back pressure is the enemy of every horsepower producing effort. You can only push so much gas through a pipe before pressure in the pipe starts rising and, to overcome this pressure, the engine has to work harder trying to push exhaust gases out of the cylinders. This state of affairs does not permit proper filling of the cylinders with fresh charge, since much of the available space is taken up by unscavenged exhaust gas. If you really want to stick with the standard system some modifications to the manifold are detailed in the engine chapter.

Owners of cars equipped with catalytic converters and electronic fuel injection systems are in some trouble here. If you keep the cat, tuning will be limited to recalibrating the CPU with tuned chips which can produce 5 per cent more power from non-turbo engines and 15 per cent from turbo engines. If you throw away the cat you can do all that's detailed here, but there may be unfortunate legal implications . . .

## Exhaust system - what you need

What is needed is a larger pipe. This, though, will only solve part of the problem because we are just a little greedy and wonder how we can manipulate things to make exhaust gases help themselves out of the engine? Well, after many years of cutting, bending and welding exhaust systems some very useful data has emerged which will help you to tailor a purpose-made system to your car or acquire the most appropriate aftermarket system.

Variables taken into account when designing exhaust systems are -

*a) Cylinder capacity*
*b) Exhaust cycle duration*

*c) Rpm requirements*

Of the three variables, the last is the most difficult to determine. I will clarify matters by saying that it is the

**4/1 Excellent quality exhaust manifolds by Shankle. Top one is for 105 Giulia coupés, Spiders and Berlinas, bottom one for 116, Alfetta and Giulietta cars.**

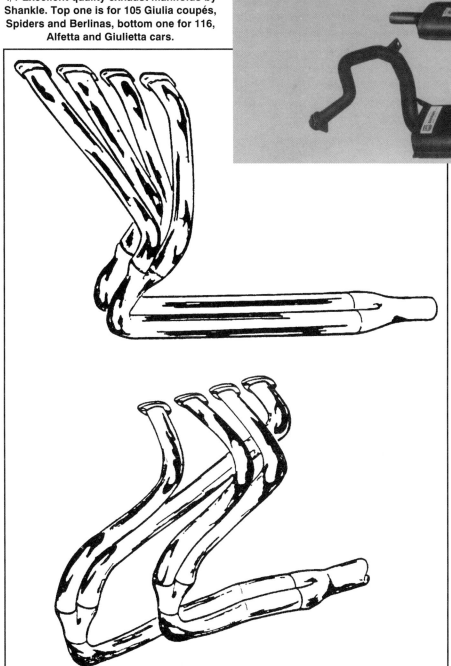

AR 1723
parte anteriore
(116.36.30.002.00)

AR 1681
4 collettori

AR 1725
parte centrale
116.36.30.015.00

AR 1727
parte posteriore
116.10.30.003.05

**4/2 Ansa exhaust system for the Alfetta GTV.**

engine speed (in rpm) at which you want the exhaust system to be at its best. Unfortunately, if the exhaust system is 'tuned' to this rpm, it means that the engine's performance will be lower everywhere else. As a matter of fact, the further away we operate from optimum rpm the lower exhaust efficiency will be . . .

You have a choice to make now as far as the favored engine speed goes. Do you want the exhaust system to be at its best at the point of highest torque or at the point of maximum power? Let me point out right away that selecting the latter is a mistake for a car used on the road. On the other hand, selecting the torque peak would leave a large gap between it and the power peak. It then seems sensible to select a point somewhere between the two for our calculation. If you expect maximum power around 6200rpm and maximum torque around 4600rpm, then it would sound right to design your system to peak at something like 5400rpm. In this case you'd need to aim for an exhaust system with four primary pipes and two intermediate pipes (4-2-1) of the dimensions detailed in the accompanying table. I'm recommending a 4-2-1 system as I know such systems fit Alfas easily and do not usually require body alterations. If you're looking for a high performance 4-1 system for more power at high revs, Rossi Engineering (UK) make a system in stainless steel which does not require body alteration.

Now that you have all this information on tube sizes and lengths, you can either have a system built to your specification, or you can pick an aftermarket system off the shelf which most nearly matches your requirements. To keep all this in perspective you should be aware that the theoretically optimized system detailed will probably be no more than 5 per cent better in terms of power output than a good commercial high performance system.

Varying system dimensions around the values tabulated is permissible and, at times, even mandatory, depending on what characteristics you want from your car. For example, decreasing primary tube diameter will help out the lower range by lowering the point at which peak torque is observed. Increasing the diameter will of course raise peak torque rpm. To quote some numbers, a 3mm (0.118in) reduction in pipe diameter will move the torque peak down by about 700-800rpm. Short primary pipes should be avoided at all cost since they greatly reduce low and mid-range torque. Note that the point of peak torque is not changed but the shape of the curve is drastically altered, as the accompanying graph shows. (4/11).

For improved road manners from the 2000, I suggest, from experience, that you decrease the secondary tube to 45mm (1.772in) inside diameter.

### 4-2-1 EXHAUST SYSTEM (FAST ROAD) - IDEAL COMPONENT DIMENSIONS -

|  | 1300 | 1600 | 1750/1800 | 2000 |
|---|---|---|---|---|
|  | ID/Length | ID/Length | ID/Length | ID/Length |
| Primary | 34x380 | 34x380 | 36x380 | 37x380 |
| Secondary | 40x500 | 42x500 | 45x550 | 48x550 |
| Final | 48(ID) | 50(ID) | 50(ID) | 52(ID) |

### 4-2-1 EXHAUST SYSTEM (RACE) - IDEAL COMPONENT DIMENSIONS -

|  | 1300 | 1600 | 1750/1800 | 2000 |
|---|---|---|---|---|
|  | ID/Length | ID/Length | ID/Length | ID/Length |
| Primary | 34x380 | 34x380 | 37x380 | 39x380 |
| Secondary | 50x500 | 50x500 | 50x550 | 52x550 |
| Final | 55(ID) | 55(ID) | 55(ID) | 55(ID) |

This will improve driveability everywhere, with minimal (indiscernible) loss high up the range.

It's very important that the pipe merging joints be properly made, otherwise the intended scavenging effect will be weakened. To keep noise down and performance up, you must use three silencers! A short one acting as an expansion chamber followed by two mufflers, one in the middle of the car's length and one at the rear. If they are of generous size they will not slow you down at all. Exhaust system detail can be seen in the accompanying drawings along with the shape of critical "Y" joints. (4/3 to 4/8).

Incidentally, you may have noticed how some standard exhaust system tubes are squeezed and deformed; where they pass over the halfshaft of 116 series cars, for instance. This is supposedly done to make the system fit; however, if you do have a system made to your specification (no matter for which

**4/3, 4, 5 & 6 These four sketches compare standard, proprietory and ideal exhaust manifolds/headers for the 116 Alfetta. Below, Standard Alfa (European) cast iron manifold has small bores and wrong lengths. Right top, Ansa type 1681 steel tube headers which have almost ideal primary bores and lengths but over-small outlet bores. Right centre, Supersprint steel headers with good primary bores but small outlet bores and wrong lengths. Right bottom, seamless steel tube headers to a proposed ideal specification: note proper pipe merging joints.**

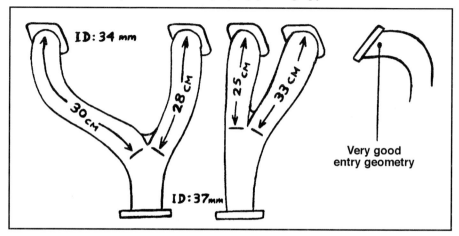

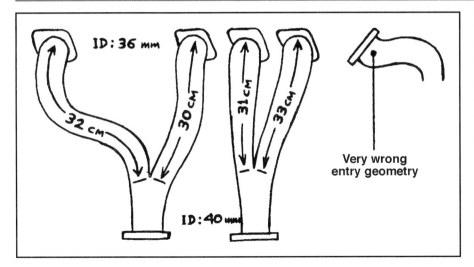

Very wrong
entry geometry

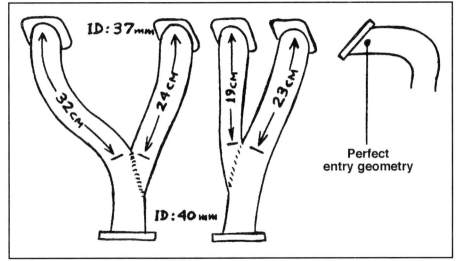

Perfect
entry geometry

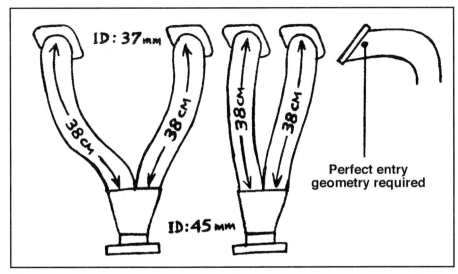

Perfect entry
geometry required

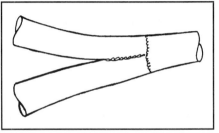

**4/7 This type of pipe joint does not fully exploit exhaust gas energy.**

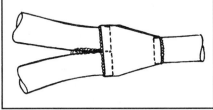

**4/8 A pipe joint designed to take advantage of gas pulse energy to a great extent.**

model) remember that it can *definitely* be made so as to fit everywhere *without* being deformed at all. Time and time again, I have seen 60mm (2.362in) outside diameter systems be cut, bent and then installed under GTVs with no fuss at all. But, then again, some jobs separate the men from the boys, don't they?

GTA headers (tubular exhaust manifolds) can be used for 105 and 115 series cars, but my feeling is that the primary pipes should really be a bit larger for the 2000 engine. Don't forget they were designed for 1600cc (and 1300) cars with the hairiest cam those days being the 101210320001. The primary tube inside diameter of these headers (Alfa part no. 105160107100 and 105160107200) is 34mm (1.339in). Primary lengths are not something to be proud of either as they are far from equal with each other. Nevertheless these headers are still much better than the standard system. The rest of the GTA system is simply excellent, though it can be hard to find new these days: try

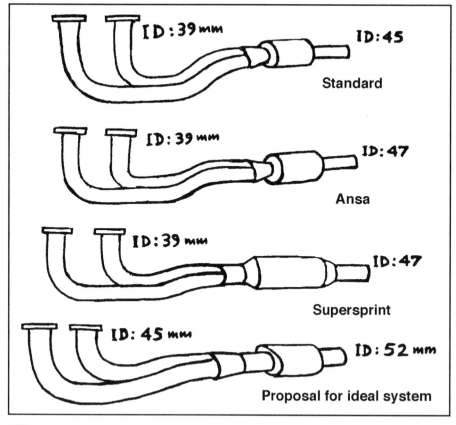

ID:39 mm    ID:45
**Standard**

ID:39 mm    ID:47
**Ansa**

ID:39 mm    ID:47
**Supersprint**

ID: 45 mm    ID: 52 mm
**Proposal for ideal system**

**4/10 Specially made for the author's Alfetta GTV this exhaust manifold has optimum lengths and diameters. Note welded reinforcing pieces to prevent stress breakage (Alfa engines rock quite a bit on their rather soft mounts).**

**4/9 Comparison of exhaust systems for 116 Alfetta. The standard system is restrictive, the Ansa system has poor pipe merging and the Supersprint system a generous expansion chamber and very good merging joint.**

Alfa specialists like EB Spares (UK).

### Exhaust system - avoiding broken tubes

One very real problem with 116 series cars is that of breaking exhaust manifolds. This is due to a poor exhaust system support arrangement. As a matter of fact, in a modified car this annoyance will repeat itself regularly, unless something is done to put things right. If a steel tubing header type exhaust manifold is installed in a 116 series car, sooner, rather than later, breakage will be experienced just behind the front expansion chamber. You see, this is now the weakest point of the system as it is no longer so easy to break the manifold itself. My short term advice in this case is to use only "U" clamps to connect the exhaust sections together: these clamps allow a little relative motion of the pipes connected, so long as they're not overtightened.

Unluckily, the more highly modified an engine is, the greater the chance of a broken exhaust pipe because, as the engine becomes more powerful, it twists more as torque is applied. This twisting motion is what breaks the exhaust tubes. If you're investing in a complete new exhaust system, as described earlier, it will be a good idea to build in a 'fix' to this problem by installing a special exhaust pipe joint just after the expansion chamber. This type of joint is standard equipment on several cars now, especially transverse engined front wheel drive ones. It allows freedom of radial motion while forming an effective gas seal. Details of the flexible joint are shown in the accompanying diagram (4/12). To have it made, you'll need the help of both a machine shop and a muffler shop.

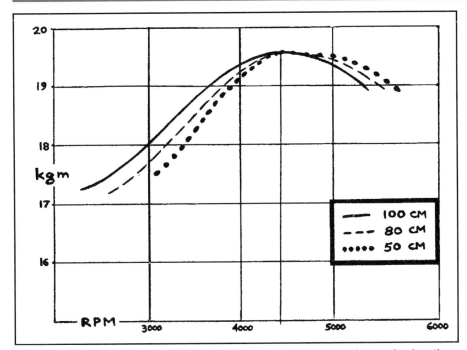

4/11 Graph illustrating typical torque curve changes relative to primary pipe length.

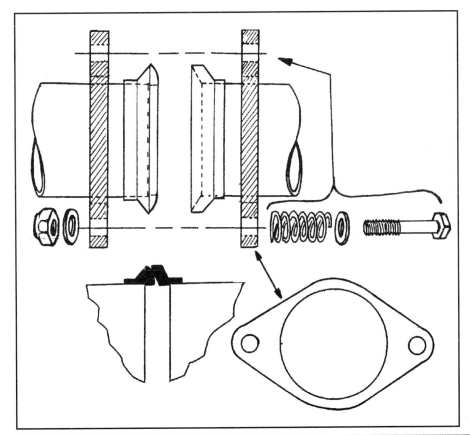

4/12 Detail of 'flexible' exhaust pipe connection. The springs allow some relative movement to occur. Nuts should be of the self-locking type.

# Chapter 5
# OIL AND WATER COOLING

Your modified engine is now completely assembled. However, there are still a few details to attend to; details which will help to ensure that the engine serves you well for a long time.

## OIL COOLING

Alfa engines (not the boxer type) are among the few blessed with high capacity oil sumps. In addition, the oil pan offers good oil cooling because it is equipped with external fins which act as heat exchangers. This is, however, not the end of oil temperature problems because, even with this arrangement, oil temperatures reach uncomfortably high levels in hot weather. Oil temperature can also be raised uncomfortably during club racing or cross-country driving. Leaving oil deterioration out, high temperatures result in lower pressure because of lowered viscosity.

To be really sure your expensive engine is as bulletproof as possible, you'll need to install an oil-cooler kit with a thermostatic valve; one that only directs oil to the cooler when the oil has reached a temperature of 85-90 degrees C (185-194 degrees F). One very important and not so obvious point here: all oil-cooling system tubing and fittings must be of at least 12.5mm (0.5in) inside diameter. Examine the block adaptor plate itself and enlarge any passages found to be smaller than the minimum. This will ensure adequate oil quantity and proper pump operation.

As far as oil is concerned I have no hard and fast rules to set, but make sure you use a good quality brand 20W50 multigrade which I've found works very well, as do most high-quality synthetic oils. I've tried synthetic 10W60 oil for racing and, so far, it looks good, although I noticed lower pressures than with the previously used 20W50 competition oil. This

lower oil pressure is normal, as lubrication quality is excellent with synthetics. During high RPM punishment both types hold up extremely well. However, all my tests are run with oil coolers installed which, in itself, is a further measure of security. Whatever oil you use change it and the filter as frequently as possible. If you're using traditional multigrade, regard Alfa's official oil change schedules as maximum periods. Those using synthetics should follow the oil manufacturer's instructions, bearing in mind that you are probably working the oil harder than would be the case in a standard car.

## WATER COOLING

The cooling system is another area requiring your attention. The original equipment thermostat is a little too "hot" for a modified engine. You should swap it for one with 74 degree C (165 degree F) markings. Have no

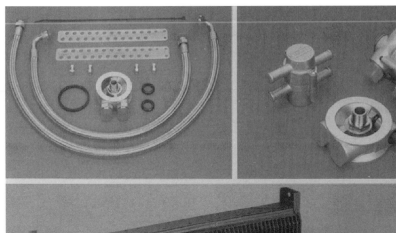

provide, there is the horsepower gain-power not wasted to drive the mechanical fan. This power gain can be up to 6bhp in the case of the 2000cc engine's large plastic fan! Electric fans, being thermostatically controlled, allow faster engine heating on cold days and, on the other hand, move more air through the radiator during idling. Use the recommended antifreeze/coolant mix to preserve cooling system integrity and to protect the alloy of the engine from internal corrosion: minerals in tap water react with the alloy in the block to form a thermal barrier film which drastically reduces heat transfer efficiency.

**5/1 Proprietary oil coolers come in all shapes and sizes together with all necessary accessories. For street and non-professional use, a 13 row cooler is enough for Alfas up to 2000cc. Nice additions are steel braided hoses and thermostatic adaptors.**

fear, your car's heater will still push out very hot air. It has been found that this temperature is optimal for a modified engine such as our project unit and, as part of the 74 degree deal, you also get lower oil temperatures.

There's a chance that in 116 series cars the radiator may prove to be a bit small for use with a modified engine. Enlarging it would be a good idea to avoid a warped cylinder head

in the summer. With some minor sheet metal alterations, you can fit the radiator from a GTV6 and end all cooling problems right away. Include both cooling fans of course.

Fortunately, 105 and 115 series cars do not seem to suffer from inadequate radiators but will still benefit from the installation of electric cooling fans. Beside the definite asset of better cooling which the electric fans

# Chapter 6
# GENERAL INFORMATION

In this chapter you'll find a variety of information of value and interest to the Alfa Romeo modifier. Where possible, factory part numbers are noted to assist you in locating parts. Unfortunately many of the parts mentioned are no longer available new, though examples will be in the hands of *Alfisti* who will not be easily parted from such gems; for instance, I would not part with a genuine GTA close ratio gearbox, nor an extremely rare set of aluminum brake calipers ... Still, you never know what you may find once you start looking. The information in this chapter is yours to enjoy and make of what you will.

## SPECIAL GEARBOX RATIOS - 105 SERIES

In contrast to the 116 series cars, there is a vast selection of gear ratios available for the 105. Let's not forget that the factory was intensely involved in racing after the TZ cars began their official careers. GTAs followed in their tracks, then GTAms, altogether accounting for about 12 years, or so, of international competition. Gearing cars is one area where an outsider's advice is not much good because the selection must cater for track parameters, engine specs, type of tires allowed and, yes, even driving style.

I'll list the gearbox ratios that have been available (along with gear part numbers), but that's about the best I can do. Don't get too excited though, there is probably very, very little chance you can obtain one, let alone all, of these special gear sets which are very rare and, usually, when finally located, are not for sale! Most of these special gear sets, originate from the 1600 and 1300GTA cars and are of special construction, as you might surmise. The gears are drilled for lightness and lower inertia - giving a small gain in countless accelerations and decelerations during a race.

If you get the chance to drive a car with these ratios, especially the one with the long 1st gear, you'll be surprised to find that downshifting to 1st is easy and fun: strange, to say the least, for an Alfa box! The accompanying table lists the very desirable gear sets that Alfa Romeo used in the 'sixties and 'seventies.

1) "Short" gearbox, lightweight gears.

| Gear | Ratio | Part number |
|------|-------|-------------|
| I. | 2.334 | 105.32.13.027.02 |
| II. | 1.576 | 105.11.13.025 00 |
| III. | 1.207 | 105.11.13.023 00 |
|  |  | +105.11.13.028.00 |
| IV. | 1 | 105.32.13.021.00 |
| V. | 0.883 | 105.11.13.031.00 |
|  |  | +105.11.13.301.00 |
| VI. | 3.01 | 105.32.13.208.00 |

2) "Close ratio" gearbox, lightweight gears

| Gear | Ratio | Part number |
|------|-------|-------------|
| I. | 2.536 | 105.32.13.027.01 |

| | | |
|---|---|---|
| II. | 1.701 | 105.32.13.025.01 |
| III. | 1.256 | 105.16.13.02.00 |
| | | +105.32.13.028.01 |
| IV. | 1 | 105.32.13.021.00 |
| V. | 0.856 | 105.16.13.031.01 |
| | | +105.32.13.301.01 |
| R | 3.01 | 105.32.13.208.00 |

3) "Intermediate" ratio gearbox, lightweight gears

| Gear | Ratio | Part number |
|---|---|---|
| I. | 2.762 | 105.32.13.027.03 |
| II. | 1.778 | 105.11.13.02.01 |
| III. | 1.304 | 105.11.13.03.01 |
| | | + 105.11.13.028.01 |
| IV. | 1 | 105.32.13.021.00 |
| V. | 0.815 | 105.11.13.021.00 |
| R | 3.01 | 105.32.13.208.0 |
| | | + 105.11.13.301.01 |

4) Standard ratios for late 105 cars (for comparison)

| Gear | Ratio | Part number |
|---|---|---|
| I. | 3.30 | 105.14.13.027.03 |
| II. | 1.99 | 105.14.13.025.03 |
| III. | 1.35 | 105.14.13.02.03 |
| | | + 105.02.13.028.00 |
| IV. | 1 | 105.14.13.021.03 |
| V. | 0.79 | 105.14.13.031.03 |
| | | + 102.00.13.301.01 |
| R. | 3.01 | 105.14.13.208.00 |

These are the various boxes used in racing for 105 cars. To some extent, there was a limited possibility for ratio mixing where necessary but this would be the exception. If you happen to find a few of the above mentioned part numbers, remember that you most probably need the complete set for a working gearbox, unless you have extraordinary machine shop capabilities - i.e. gear cutting. Someone who knows boxes well can combine some lightweight gears with standard gears and come up with a usable 'Frankenstein' box! In this case,

### FINAL DRIVE GEAR SETS (105 SERIES CARS)

| Ratio | # Teeth | Stock Pt.No. | Lightweight Pt.No. |
|---|---|---|---|
| 3.73 | 11/41 | 105.16.17.021.00 | None |
| 3.91 | 11/43 | None | 105.32.17.021.05 |
| 4.10 | 10/41 | 105.14.17.021.01 | 105.32.17.021.02 |
| 4.56 | 9/41 | 105.00.17.021.03 | 105.32.17.021.00 |
| 4.78 | 9/43 | 105.16.17.021.01 | 105.32.17.021.01 |
| 5.12 | 8/41 | 102.02.17.021.01 | None |
| 5.38 | 8/43 | None | 105.32.17.021.04 |
| 5.86 | 7/41 | None | 105.32.17.021.03 |

a lot of thought must go into the intended shift points along with appropriate rpm and speed calculations.

## DIFFERENTIAL - 105 SERIES CARS

105 series cars had the luxury of a large selection of gear sets for their final drives. Between "stock" and "racing only" sets, virtually any competition situation could be catered for. The factory's commitment to competition was such that it even supplied hollow pinion and lightweight ring gears! I have tabulated the original ratios along with the relevant part numbers in the accompanying table.

A limited-slip-differential, or LSD for short, is a must for any kind of fast driving. As a matter of fact, it was standard equipment on all 2000cc 105 and 115 cars. For those of you who want one of these units, forget about fitting one to your old non-LSD axles, unless you are a very knowledgeable masochist - it just isn't worth the trouble. Find a wrecked 2000 car and remove the whole axle. It's very difficult to convert an old axle, and equally difficult to change gears (ring and pinion) in any axle. The operation requires precision and expensive

instruments to set bearing preloads and other vital clearances. These exacting operations are necessary if you plan to keep your axle for many thousands of miles instead of a week or two - which is how long it will last if crudely assembled by a seat-of-the-pants method.

Factory LSDs came in two ratios: 4.1 for the GTV and Spider and 4.3 for the Berlina four-door. Both types had a 25% lockout ratio. However, it's fairly easy to modify this ratio to a more raceworthy and exhilarating 47%. All you have to do is disassemble the axle (remember to drain all oil before taking the unit apart!). Then, reassemble the unit after substituting two 'cross'-shaped washer plates with two friction plates: the overall thickness of the 'innards' must remain the same. For the record, the Montreal also came standard with a 4.1 ratio LSD, plus a very nice cooler for the differential oil which was unique in the Giulia range. An added Montreal bonus is the rear vented disc brakes, making this car's axle a very desirable find!

Owners of smaller engined cars who wish to have a LSD, but feel the 4.1 or 4.3 ratios are inappropriate for their cars, will have to consult a specialist engineer to see what the possibilities are for marrying other

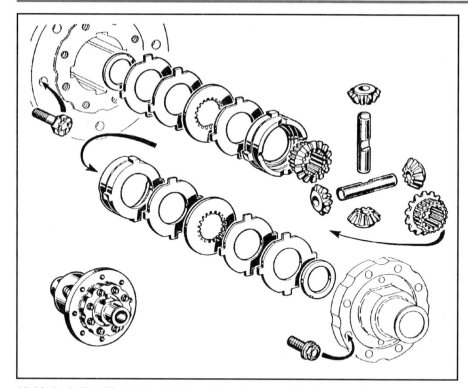

**6/1 Limited-slip-differential of 2000cc 105-series cars. Note that not all parts interchange with 116 series LSD transaxles.**

limited slip differential to boot. And all this of course is coupled to the new improved (since 1985) shift linkage system. Performance seekers should be very satisfied with the new transaxles. For those who want something more, however, a true racing set of gears is available from sources outside the factory.

The accompanying table shows the information I have compiled on gearsets.

|     | Early 116 | Late 116 | 75TS & Turbo | Special Race |
|-----|-----------|----------|--------------|--------------|
| I   | 3.3       | 3.5      | 2.875        | 2.57         |
| II  | 1.99      | 1.956    | 1.72         | 1.94         |
| III | 1.35      | 1.258    | 1.226        | 1.55         |
| IV  | 1.04      | 0.946    | 0.946        | 1.21         |
| V   | 0.83      | 0.78     | 0.78         | 1.0          |

For racing purposes LSD units can be had with up to a 75% lockout ratio. For those who feel lucky, the original ZF LSD unit part number used in the GTV 1800 options is 116.08.17.043.01. This differential, as well as the ones used in the 75TS and Turbo models, can be modified for

ratios to the LSD set-up.

## TRANSAXLE - 116 SERIES CARS

When the first Alfetta 1800 GTs appeared they could be had with the optional ZF 25% LSD (limited slip differential), very similar but not identical to the one common to some of the Giulia 105 models. However, after a very brief period, the option was discontinued and disappeared from subsequent parts lists. My guess is that the very well balanced character of the Alfetta cars persuaded the factory that such options were not necessary, especially as these cars were aimed at an older age group than the earlier Giulia ('Bertone') GTs.

Fortunately, the factory has helped enthusiasts immensely by coming out with the 75 Twin Spark

and the 75 turbo cars. Not only have Alfa changed the gear ratios to sporty looking sets, they've also included a

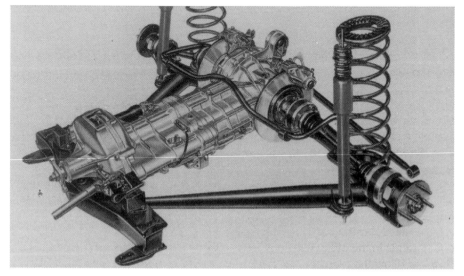

**6/2 Famous, effective, elaborate and expensive (all four): the transaxle and de Dion-type rear suspension of 116 series cars. Improved versions of this set-up were used in the SZ and ES30 cars.**

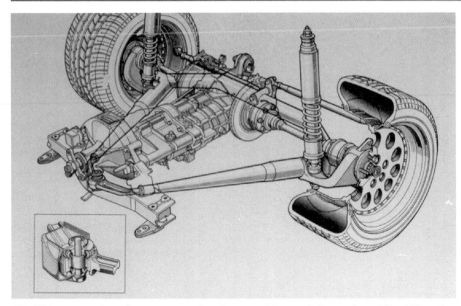

**6/3 ES30 transaxle and rear suspension: improved heavy-duty version of the 116-series unit.**

47% ratio easily enough. Note that not all internal parts interchange with the Giulia LSD units.

## STEERING RATIOS

You are all well aware of the very slow steering ratio rack and pinion system in the 116 series cars.

Fortunately, the TAR-OX company markets a system that transforms your 3.6 turns lock-to-lock into a very comfortable 2.5 turn system. I have been using this in my own GTV for eight years now and I wouldn't have it any other way. You can buy the complete steering unit or just the rack and pinion components themselves to save money. However, if you go this way note that the new components will only fit the original Spica unit and not the ZF unit, so check what's fitted to your car. Adjustment of the new components in the old unit is very simple. Follow the rebuild procedures outlined in the appropriate repair manuals. A wheel alignment will of course be required when all is done.

For club competition use, I suggest you install a smaller diameter steering wheel in addition to the above, and your car will feel and turn very much like a real racer. However, you can't have everything; be prepared for some effort when parking or otherwise maneuvering the car. Using the quick steering unit with the standard wheel will be excellent for all-round use.

105 series cars are more difficult to improve. Factory parts were once available to quicken the steering ratio, now you'll have to rely on specialists to help you with parts. A smaller steering wheel will of course be of help in guiding your four-wheel pet around curves. Be aware though, that a small steering wheel makes the steering feel heavier. In fact, a quick steering ratio combined with a small diameter steering wheel and fat tires will give you a very difficult time during tight parking maneuvers, especially when combined with negative camber up front.

A more radical approach for 105-series owners is to fit a rack & pinion unit. You'll need some engineering expertise, but it can be done and will give a weight saving of around 5 kilos (11lb).

## SUSPENSION - 105 SERIES CARS

Most owners with a faster than usual 105 install aftermarket adjustable shock absorbers such as Koni, Spax, etc, with good results. Harder springs and thicker stabilizer bars are available from Alfa specialists. However, it must be said that for most road use the 105 suspension is pretty good in standard form as it is more of a driver's car than the Alfetta range.

However, for seriously fast drivers, a dramatic improvement in handling can be made by duplicating Autodelta's treatment of the front upper control arms. What Autodelta did was to interpose special 'knuckle risers' between the top of the spindles and the control arms and, at the same time, used longer, specially made, control arms to cater for the new position of the upper ball joint. Using two spherical (Heim) bearings to replace the two rubber bushings in the control arms completed the transformation. As a consequence of these modifications, the cars had pronounced negative front wheel camber during cornering, resulting in better handling altogether. The necessary parts to effect this transformation are:

*Knuckle risers:*     *105.32.21.118.00*
*Control arms (L/R): 105.32.21.026.01*
                   *and*
            *105.32.21.027.02*
*Bumper extensions: 105.32.21.744.00*

Note that racing GTAs front wheels usually had 1-2 degrees - occasionally as much as 3-3.5 degrees

- of negative camber (depending on tires used) as compared with the stock model's 0.5-1.5 degrees of positive camber.

For cars that don't have a rear stabilizer (anti-roll) bar, a worthwhile conversion can be effected by installing all relevant bits and pieces from a 1750 or 2000 Giulia. Parts can still be found in breaker's yards and therefore need cost very little. Fit new rubber bushings (they're cheap) before installing the stabilizer bar.

Perhaps the most noted historical modification in the suspension of 105 cars was the 'sliding block' rear end used in some GTAs. This set-up lowered the car's rear roll center by about 150mm (6in) or so, resulting in a dramatic handling improvement. However, the system was rather complicated and was not universally admired: building the equivalent today would be prohibitively expensive.

Not as rare as the sliding block system, but prized nonetheless, is the aluminum torque "Tee" which replaces the original heavy cast iron unit in all 105 rear suspensions, reducing high rear weight. Alfa part number is 105.32.25.003.01

The experienced engineer can consider building an Alfetta-type Watts linkage or even a Panhard rod system using tubing and joints of appropriate quality.

## SUSPENSION - 116 SERIES CARS

As the Alfetta series was originally presented, the cars were very softly sprung and exhibited pronounced body roll when cornering. Vehicle balance was, luckily, not a problem, perhaps predictably enough when remembering the almost 50/50 weight distribution.

This exaggerated softness and body roll was severely criticized and the factory finally began to react in 1980 by fitting firmer suspension components to the cars.

Here's a list of various suspension components and their sizes -

1) Front stabilizer (anti-roll) bars
| | |
|---|---|
| 18mm - | 116102160000 |
| 20mm - | 116552160000 |
| 22mm - | 116002160012 |
| 24mm - | 116812160000 |
| 27mm - | Shankle Pt. No. 4705 |
| 28mm - | Romeo Racing Pt. No. 026025 |

Renew all bushings and use center pieces with correct inside diameter for the job. Depending on vehicle use, you may have to reinforce the sheet metal where the front brackets are.

2) Torsion bars (L + R)
| | |
|---|---|
| 18.4mm - | 116102150500 + 116102150600 |
| 19.5mm - | 116562150500 + 116552150600 |
| 21.1mm - | 116912150500 + 116362150600 |
| 22.1mm - | 116422150500 + 116422150600 |
| 23.4mm - | 116592150600 + 116602150500 |
| 25.4mm - | Shankle Pt. No. 4711 |

A variety of torsion bars (up to 39mm thick) is available from Romeo Racing. As far as adjustment goes suit yourself regarding the proper ride height.

3) Rear stabilizer bars
| | |
|---|---|
| 20mm - | 116002508410 |
| 22mm - | 116432560000 |
| 24mm - | 113582560000 |

There are two types of mounting arrangements used here, so check your car to see whether you need any additional parts. There is no problem converting from one system to the other.

4) Springs
| | |
|---|---|
| Standard - | 116102551001 |
| Reinforced - | 116342551000 |
| Heavy Duty - | 116462551004 |
| Extra Heavy Duty - | 113582551000 |
| | Shankle p.n. 4710 |

A variety of springs is available from Romeo Racing and others for all kinds of requirements. Some may have to lose one or, at the most, two coils to adjust ride height, but keep in mind that when springs are shortened the result is a different spring altogether - a stiffer one.

For various applications you may want to use these ride-height adjusting spacers - 116002552805 with 7mm of thickness; 116002552806 with 14mm of thickness; 116002552807 with 21mm of thickness. These are standard factory items.

## BRAKES

Contrary to popular belief, there is a lot that can be done to improve even a four-wheel disc brake system like the Alfa's.

For fast road use the cheapest improvement is a set of high-performance pads, though they'll require more pedal pressure. There was a large choice of performance pads in the days when pads had a high asbestos content, but today's ecological requirements have narrowed down the available selection.

The next step after pads is a set of special front discs, grooved or bimetal such as the ones marketed by Tarox. At this stage, teflon brake hoses are a must, as is very good quality brake fluid to DOT 5 specification available from a number of manufacturers.

For serious competition, brake cooling ducts are necessary, along with fresh brake fluid for every race. It should go without saying that calipers must be in perfect condition. Owners of 116 series cars may consider fitting 5-bolt wheels and related hardware from the GTV6, A75 3000cc and others which have ventilated discs up front. If you're really lucky, you might come across some four-pot calipers like the ones used in the Giulietta Turbodelta, but they're rare.

105 owners will find that it's possible to fit Montreal vented discs on Veloce models (and, perhaps, others) with which the aluminum Brembo calipers from a GTV6 or 75 should be used. To get all this behind 13 inch wheels some careful mounting of the calipers will be necessary as well as judicious filing of caliper protrusions.

Owners of 105 cars can search (forever, I'm afraid) for the GTAm

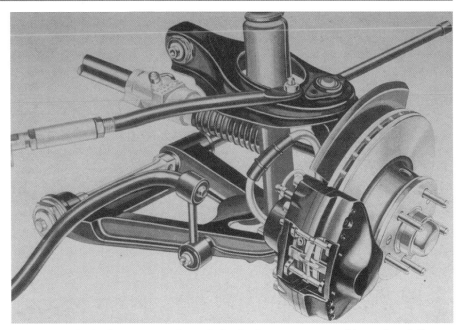

6/5 75 1.8 Turbo front suspension. 5-bolt wheels separate cars with ventilated discs from others.

6/4 Brake component testing is serious business at Tarox (Lecco, Italy). Owner Gianni Taroni offers only bulletproof brake equipment. Testing is taken to extremes as seen here. Flywheel in background simulates vehicle weight (inertia). The company supplies grooved or bimetallic discs, special pads and fluid - all you need!

vented brakes of 1970 and 71. For interested parties, here are the part numbers for the 13in wheel GTAm ventilated front discs and aluminum calipers: 105.33.22.052.00 ATE aluminum caliper, right; 105.33.22.053.00 ATE aluminum caliper, left; 105.32.22.251.99 vented disc, 250mm (9.8in). ATE alloy rear calipers carry the part number 105 32 26 215 98 and it's believed that they were used with standard discs.

## TURBOCHARGING

Alfa Romeo was one of the last car manufacturers to offer turbocharged models in recent years. The A75 1800 Turbo started out in the mid-'80s with 155 horsepower and evolved to 165 after a series of minute modifications. This engine uses the Bosch L-Jetronic fuel injection system, along with wastegate control and rpm limiter to preserve its mechanical integrity.

It's very easy to modify turbo engines for more power, simply by raising boost pressure, however, doing so reliably is another story! In European homologated form, 212-215bhp is possible from this engine with "Group N" mods, some "legal" and a few "illegal." However, and this is a tribute to the sound basic design of the engine, in the Italian Championship "Superturismo A1" class, a staggering 400bhp has been seen! To achieve this power level more than a simple "chip" change was involved and, if you've ever had the fascinating chance to look closely inside the engine bay of one of these beasts, you'll know that the words "extensive modifications" can only begin to describe what you see!

Owners of A75 Turbo cars can readily find power upgrade kits in the market mostly consisting of reprogrammed chips and revised waste gate control. With such mods power will approach 190bhp. Further mods involving "selecting" a turbocharger with optimized characteristics can bring power to around 200bhp.

Changing to a T4 Turbo unit (instead of the original Garrett T3) and suitable cams can yield much more power but, unfortunately, this is coupled with pronounced turbo-lag lower in the rev range.

I started this section with the A75 Turbo because this car was intended to be a regular mass produced turbocharged model. In fact, as early as 1979 the factory came up with the GTV Turbodelta (Turbo Autodelta) which had a 2000 engine, Dellorto carburetors and a KKK Turbo. "Street power" of this homologation special was 150bhp, while in race trim it approached 300! These cars are very rare today to say the least. After the GTV Turbodelta came the Giulietta Turbodelta, with 175bhp on tap and a

6/6 Twin oil-driven vane superchargers squeezed out 220bhp at 7500rpm from this special 1600 GTA-SA engine in 1969. Very few were made, all for racing use. What you cannot see in the picture are the two Weber DCOEs behind the airtight air box. Ten cars were made in 1967-68 but development ceased because of inability to smooth out power progression and delivery problems.

turbo made by Alfa Romeo Avio, the company's aeronautical division. These cars are rare also, but not as rare as the GTV turbos. However, both types can be found occasionally by scouring through Italian specialist magazine and newspaper ads. The above two models saw a limited amount of racing, curtailed finally by oil-crisis related problems combined

6/7 The ultimate Alfa 4-cylinder turbo: 1500cc Formula 1 engine of 1984. Turbo unit is almost half the engine size! Exhaust manifold is a plumber's nightmare!

**6/8 75 1.8 Turbo in its natural resting place. Nice large intercooler helps power production.**

with factory policy changes.

The next engine Alfa turbocharged was the 2000 V6 as used in the 164 model. This excellent engine, deriving from the 2000 V6 of the early '80s, produces 205bhp in stock form, endowing the 164 with exhilarating performance. The four-cylinder turbocharged 1995cc engine used in the 155 Q4 is of Fiat origin and, as such, remains outside the scope of this book. In the USA, the GTV6 2.5 liter engine has been fitted, with meticulous attention to detail, with twin-turbos by Callaway Engineering: results were excellent.

Various successful attempts have been made to turbocharge the Alfa dohc in carbureted 2000 form. I believe the first one to be offered for sale as a complete kit was a Shankle product which produced a healthy 203bhp. The kit was very comprehensive, even containing special forged pistons to lower the engine's CR to

7.8:1. An unusual aspect of this conversion was that the set-up used a single horizontal twin-choke progressive throttle carburetor mounted on a proprietary manifold to feed the engine. Well, everything worked out fine, and the engine proved its worth in everyday use. Subsequent teardowns revealed no detriment to any components other than normal wear and tear.

In England, noted Alfa dealer Bell and Colvill perfected a turbo version of the carbureted 2000cc engine with Dellorto carbs. They went a step further, offering new cars with these turbo engines as an option, warranty and all. A few thousand miles away from England - quite a few actually - in Australia, Alfa Romeo dealer Beninca Motors tried their hand at turbocharging the venerable 2000 with excellent results.

If you're serious about turbocharging an Alfa engine that was

not originally so equipped, you'll need either to adapt components from an Alfa turbo set-up or use one of the many excellent aftermarket turbo kits now available for various applications. Many of the gas flowing improvements detailed in this book will still be of benefit, but you'll need to take the turbo kit manufacturer's advice on compression ratios, cams, timing, etc, because forced induction is a whole different ball game.

## ROLL CAGE

Obviously the main point of a roll cage is to protect the car's occupants in the event of a roll. However, while it may not seem obvious at first, a roll cage has every right to be considered as an important part of the car's suspension. This assembly stiffens the chassis, improving handling across the board but especially during transitions. All of this applies also to spiders (convertibles) which tend to be less stiff bodily though, for obvious reasons, are more often fitted with a roll bar, rather than a full cage.

Chassis flexing is reduced in proportion to the strength of the roll cage so great care is taken in designing them. Car behavior is optimized by small changes in the cage's component sizes and placement. Naturally, nowadays, much of this work is performed using appropriate specially developed computer programs.

Roll cages were at one time available in aluminum or steel, but recent regulation changes preclude the use of aluminum cages in most racing classes.

I recommend you fit a roll cage whenever possible for enhanced safety and better handling. Most usual for fast road and occasional racing use in sedans (saloons) and coupes is the six-point type cage with removable rear diagonal to allow for rear seat use when required. As far as spiders are concerned, the more extensive the roll cage the better, though even a single braced rear hoop will improve chassis stiffness.

You can get top quality roll cages in both steel and aluminum from firms like Matter in Germany and Sparco in Italy amongst others. Keep in mind that the original sun visors (or shields) will have to be removed to allow

installation of a full cage and some alternative means of glare protection will have to be found.

## BODY SEAM STRENGTHENING

If you desire the ultimate in chassis stiffness, you can have your car's body fully spot welded or seam-brazed by a chassis specialist. Be aware though,

that such work could affect the performance of crumple-zones designed-in by the manufacturer and is therefore undesirable for any car used on the road.

My advice for fast road and club competition use is a good inspection of existing spot and seam welds, along with the installation of a six-point roll cage.

# Appendix 1
# SUPPLIERS & SPECIALISTS

## SUPPLIERS & SPECIALISTS

Please note that we have endeavored to make this list as comprehensive as possible at the time of publication. However, you should be aware that 'phone numbers and addresses change periodically so, if you're having problems making contact with a supplier, check with directory services or your Alfa club. Listing does not imply endorsement or recommendation of any of the suppliers.

**ALBERT**
Worgl, Tyrol, AUSTRIA
Tel: 05332-2483
(Camshafts and valve train components)

**ALDON AUTOMOTIVE LTD**
Breener Industrial Estate, Station Drive, Brierley Hill, West Midlands, GREAT BRITAIN
Tel: 01384 78508
(Authorised Weber-Alpha installation specialists. Modified distributors)

**ALQUATI**
Via Dante 91, Cremona, ITALY
Tel: 393372 410398
Fax: 39372 457538
(Camshafts, exhaust systems, racing gear sets, LSD units)

**AUTOMEO**
36 Gypsy Patch Lane, Little Stoke, Bristol, GREAT BRITAIN
TEL: 01272 695771
(Maintenance & performance tuning)

**BROOKSIDE GARAGE**
55 High Street, Wrestlingworth, Sandy, Bedfordshire, GREAT BRITAIN
Tel: 01767 23217
(Restoration, maintenance & performance tuning)

**COLOMBO AND BARIANI**
Via Lazzati 4, 20154 Milano, ITALY
Tel: 392 341201
Fax: 392 341206
(Wide range of camshafts)

**E.B. SPARES**
31 Link Road, West Wilts Trading Estate, Westbury, Wiltshire BA13 4JB, GREAT BRITAIN
Tel: 01373 823856
Fax: 01373 858327
(Wide range standard and performance parts)

**GOZZOLI AUTOTRASFORMAZIONI**
Via Claudia 211, Maranello, ITALY
Tel: 39536 941240
Fax: 39536 945708
(Cams, oversize valves, high compression pistons, exhaust manifolds, dynamometer facility)

**HALTECH E.F.I.**
3121 Benton St. Garland, Texas, USA
Tel: 214 831 9800
Fax: 214 831 9802
(Programmable electronic fuel injection systems)

**BRIAN HAMMOND**
Station Cottage, Thuxton, Dereham, Norfolk, GREAT BRITAIN
TEL: 01362 850320
(Sales, maintenance & performance tuning)

**PETER HILLIARD & SON**
41 High Street, Penge, London SE20 7HJ, GREAT BRITAIN
Tel: 0181 778 5755
(Maintenance & performance tuning)

**B. HOLZ ELECTRONIK**
Heisenberg Strasse 8, 50126 Bergheim 1, GERMANY
Tel: 2271 65250
Fax: 2271 64203
(ECU reprogramming and construction for cars with EFI)

**INTERNATIONAL AUTO PARTS**
Rt. 29 North, Charlottesville VA. 22906. USA
Tel: 804 973 2892
(Wide range of special Alfa parts)

**KENT PERFORMANCE CAMS LTD**
Units 1-4, Military Road, Shorncliffe Industrial Estate, Folkestone, Kent CT20 3SP, GREAT BRITAIN
Tel: 01303 248666
Fax: 01303 252508
(Camshafts and special valve springs)

**ALWYN KERSHAW**
Chessingham Park, Dunnington, York YO1 5SE, GREAT BRITAIN
Tel: 01904 488778
(Sales, maintenance & performance tuning)

**LUMENITION**
Autocar Equipment Ltd.,
77-85 Newington Causeway, London SE1 6BJ, GREAT BRITAIN
Tel: 0171 4034334
Fax: 0171 3781270
(Programmable electronic fuel injection systems. Electronic ignition systems and advance modules)

**ROMEO RACING**
Via 24 maggio 1, ang.viale marelli, 20099 Sesto S.Giovanni, Milano, ITALY
Tel & fax: 02 2440071
(Everything special for Alfas. Full range of items)

**ROSSI ENGINEERING**
(Rob Giordanelli)
85 Vicarage Road, Sunbury-on-Thames, Middlesex TW16 7QD, GREAT BRITAIN.
Tel & Fax: 01932 786819

(Performance tuning, race preparation & repairs)

## Dr SCHRICK GMBH
Dreherstrasse 3-5, D-5630 Ramschied 11, GERMANY
Fax: 2191 561315
(Camshafts, valve springs and valve train components)

## SHANKLE AUTOMOTIVE ENGINEERING/ALFA RICAMBI
Automotive Systems Group Inc., 6644 San Fernando Road, Glendale, CA 91201, USA
Tel: 800 225 2532 (toll free)
Tel: 818 956 7933
Fax: 818 956 5160
(Wide range of standard & performance parts, plus engine preparation)

## SPERRY VALVE WORKS
2829 Gundry Avenue, Signal Hill, CA 90806, USA
Tel: 310 988 5960
(Performance tuning, especially heads)

## SPRINT FILTER
Via Giuspeppe Govone 96, Milano 20155, ITALY
Tel: 392315582
Fax: 392375697
(Carburetor air horns and air boxes)

## TAR-OX
Galbiate, Como, ITALY
Tel: 341 540870
Fax: 341 541642
(Special brake systems, modified rack and pinion sets, competition brake discs and brake pads)

## JOHN TIMPANY
20 Jason Close, Brentwood, Essex, GREAT BRITAIN
Tel: 01277 211296
(Performance tuning)

## WARD & DEANE RACING
115 N. Oak St, Inglewood, CA 90301, USA
Tel: 213 754 6008
(Performance parts, especially suspension)

## TOM ZAT
11 Zagato Lane, Aniwa, WI 54408, USA.
Tel 715 449 2141
(Huge selection of used/rare Alfa parts)

# Appendix 2
# CAMSHAFT PERFORMANCE GRAPHS

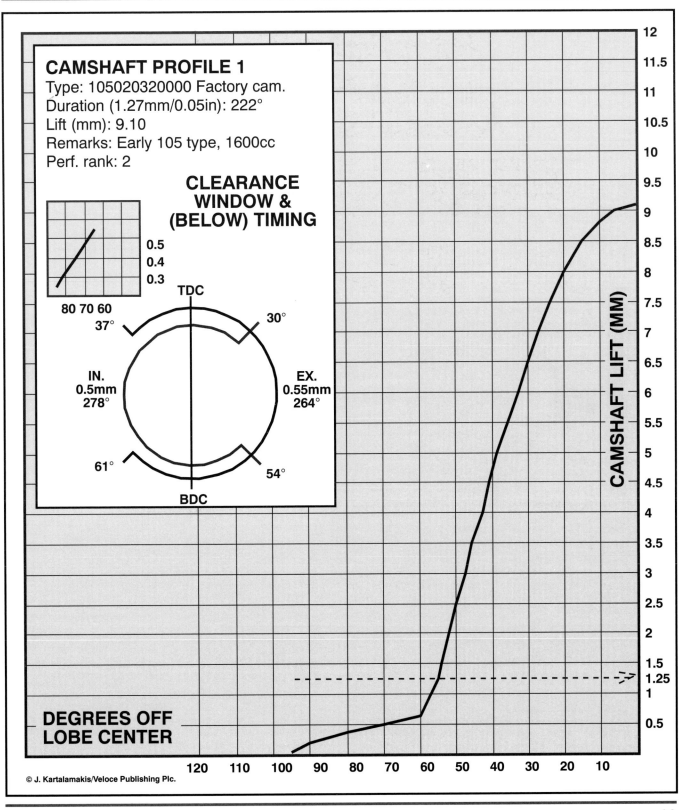

## CAMSHAFT PROFILE 1
Type: 105020320000 Factory cam.
Duration (1.27mm/0.05in): 222°
Lift (mm): 9.10
Remarks: Early 105 type, 1600cc
Perf. rank: 2

### CLEARANCE WINDOW & (BELOW) TIMING

0.5
0.4
0.3

80 70 60

TDC

37°          30°

IN.          EX.
0.5mm        0.55mm
278°         264°

61°          54°

BDC

DEGREES OFF LOBE CENTER

CAMSHAFT LIFT (MM)

120  110  100  90  80  70  60  50  40  30  20  10

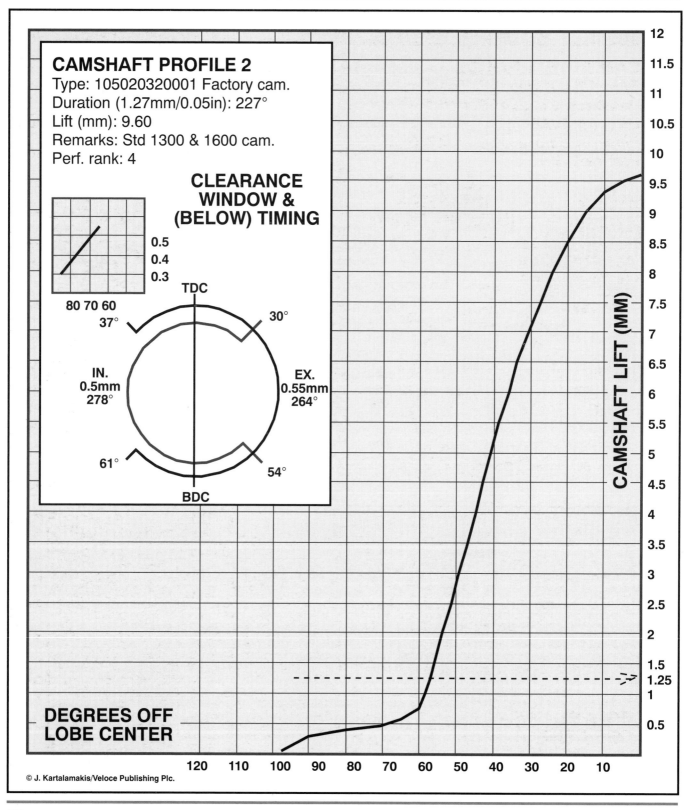

**CAMSHAFT PROFILE 2**
Type: 105020320001 Factory cam.
Duration (1.27mm/0.05in): 227°
Lift (mm): 9.60
Remarks: Std 1300 & 1600 cam.
Perf. rank: 4

**CLEARANCE WINDOW & (BELOW) TIMING**

0.5
0.4
0.3

80 70 60

37°          30°

IN.
0.5mm
278°

EX.
0.55mm
264°

61°          54°

TDC

BDC

IN. / EX. timing diagram

**DEGREES OFF LOBE CENTER**

CAMSHAFT LIFT (MM)

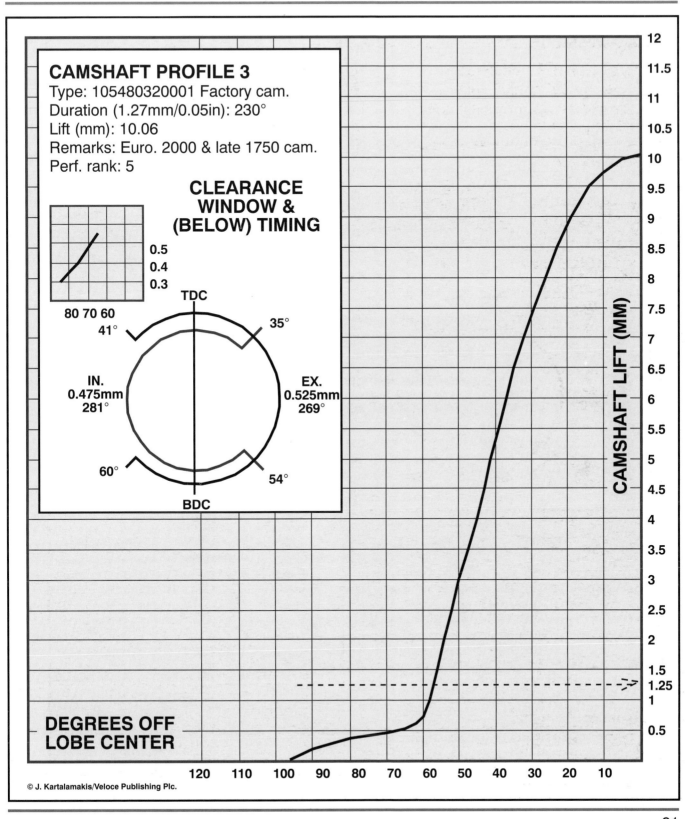

## CAMSHAFT PROFILE 3
Type: 105480320001 Factory cam.
Duration (1.27mm/0.05in): 230°
Lift (mm): 10.06
Remarks: Euro. 2000 & late 1750 cam.
Perf. rank: 5

### CLEARANCE WINDOW & (BELOW) TIMING

0.5
0.4
0.3

80 70 60
41°

TDC

35°

IN.
0.475mm
281°

EX.
0.525mm
269°

60°

54°

BDC

CAMSHAFT LIFT (MM)

DEGREES OFF LOBE CENTER

1.25

120 110 100 90 80 70 60 50 40 30 20 10

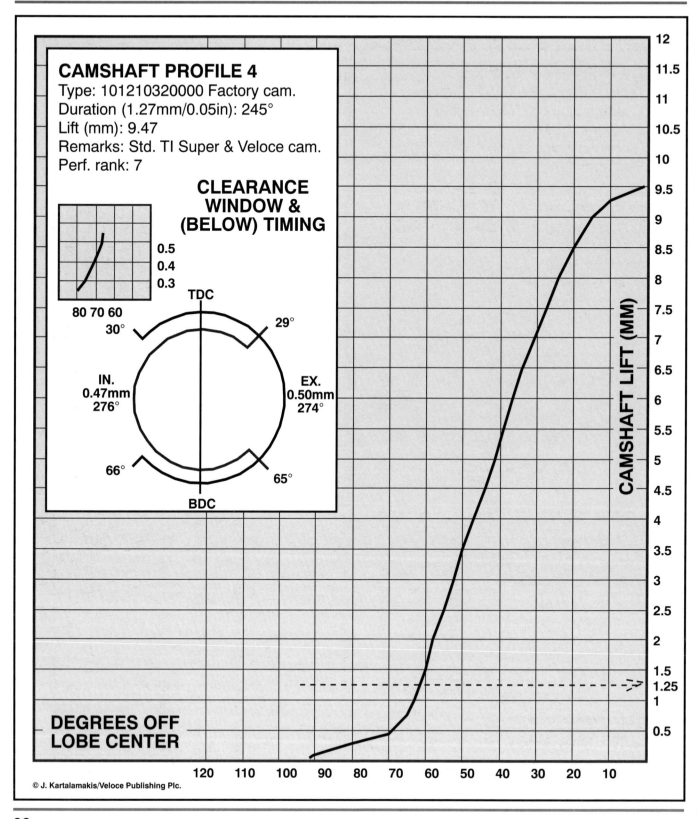

## CAMSHAFT PROFILE 4
Type: 101210320000 Factory cam.
Duration (1.27mm/0.05in): 245°
Lift (mm): 9.47
Remarks: Std. TI Super & Veloce cam.
Perf. rank: 7

### CLEARANCE WINDOW & (BELOW) TIMING

0.5
0.4
0.3

80 70 60

TDC

30°          29°

IN.
0.47mm
276°

EX.
0.50mm
274°

66°          65°

BDC

**DEGREES OFF LOBE CENTER**

CAMSHAFT LIFT (MM)

1.25

120 110 100 90 80 70 60 50 40 30 20 10

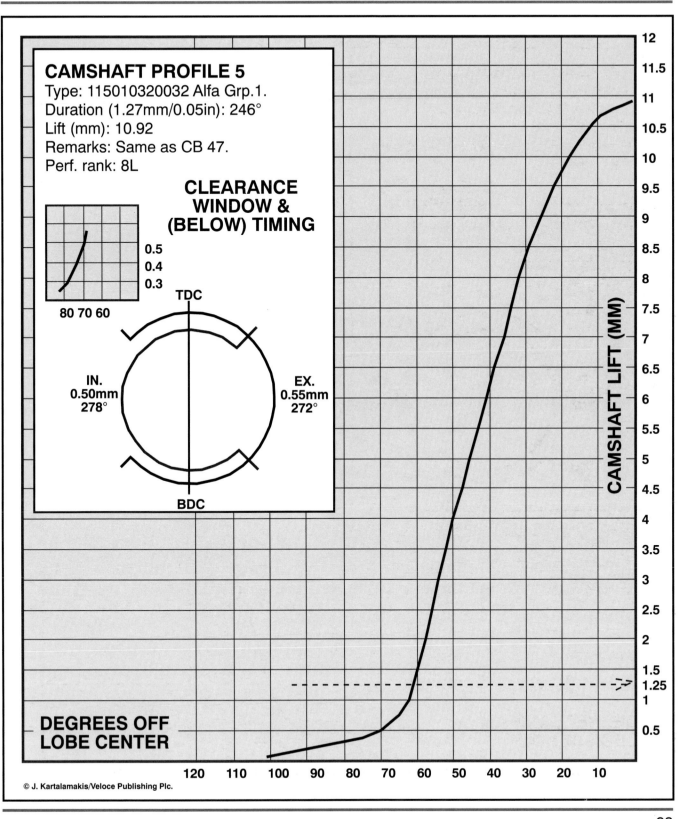

## CAMSHAFT PROFILE 5
Type: 115010320032 Alfa Grp.1.
Duration (1.27mm/0.05in): 246°
Lift (mm): 10.92
Remarks: Same as CB 47.
Perf. rank: 8L

### CLEARANCE WINDOW & (BELOW) TIMING

0.5
0.4
0.3

80 70 60

TDC

IN.
0.50mm
278°

EX.
0.55mm
272°

BDC

CAMSHAFT LIFT (MM)

DEGREES OFF
LOBE CENTER

120 110 100 90 80 70 60 50 40 30 20 10

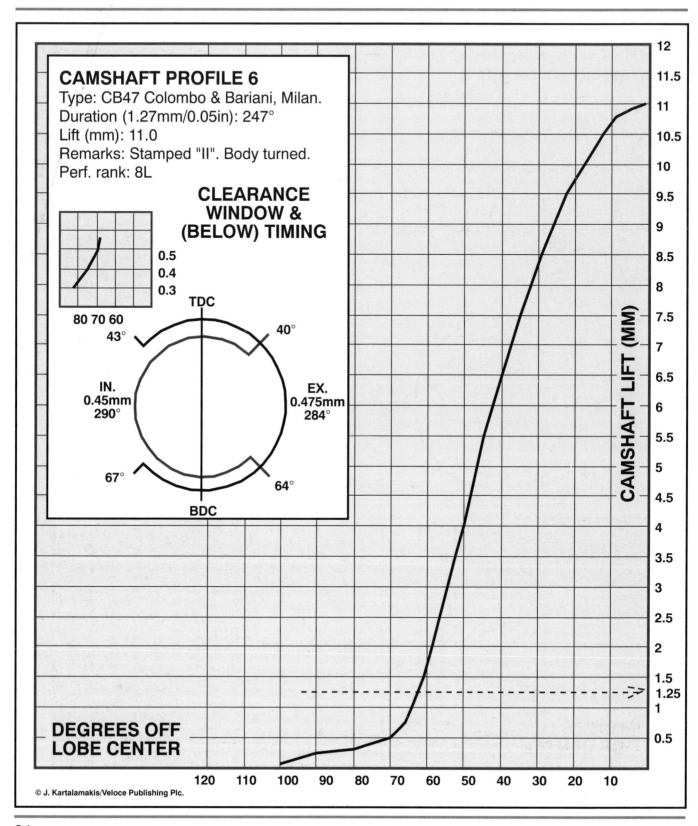

**CAMSHAFT PROFILE 6**
Type: CB47 Colombo & Bariani, Milan.
Duration (1.27mm/0.05in): 247°
Lift (mm): 11.0
Remarks: Stamped "II". Body turned.
Perf. rank: 8L

**CLEARANCE WINDOW & (BELOW) TIMING**

0.5
0.4
0.3

80 70 60

TDC

43°        40°

IN.            EX.
0.45mm         0.475mm
290°           284°

67°        64°

BDC

**DEGREES OFF LOBE CENTER**

CAMSHAFT LIFT (MM)

120  110  100  90  80  70  60  50  40  30  20  10

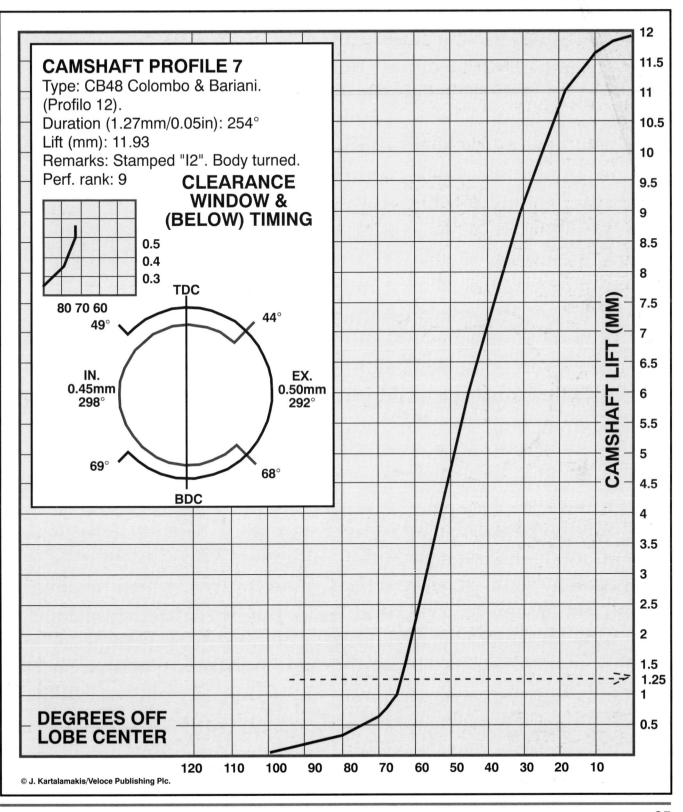

**CAMSHAFT PROFILE 7**

Type: CB48 Colombo & Bariani.
(Profilo 12).
Duration (1.27mm/0.05in): 254°
Lift (mm): 11.93
Remarks: Stamped "I2". Body turned.
Perf. rank: 9

**CLEARANCE WINDOW & (BELOW) TIMING**

0.5
0.4
0.3

80 70 60

TDC

49°          44°

IN.          EX.
0.45mm       0.50mm
298°         292°

69°          68°

BDC

**DEGREES OFF LOBE CENTER**

CAMSHAFT LIFT (MM)

12
11.5
11
10.5
10
9.5
9
8.5
8
7.5
7
6.5
6
5.5
5
4.5
4
3.5
3
2.5
2
1.5
1.25
1
0.5

120  110  100  90  80  70  60  50  40  30  20  10

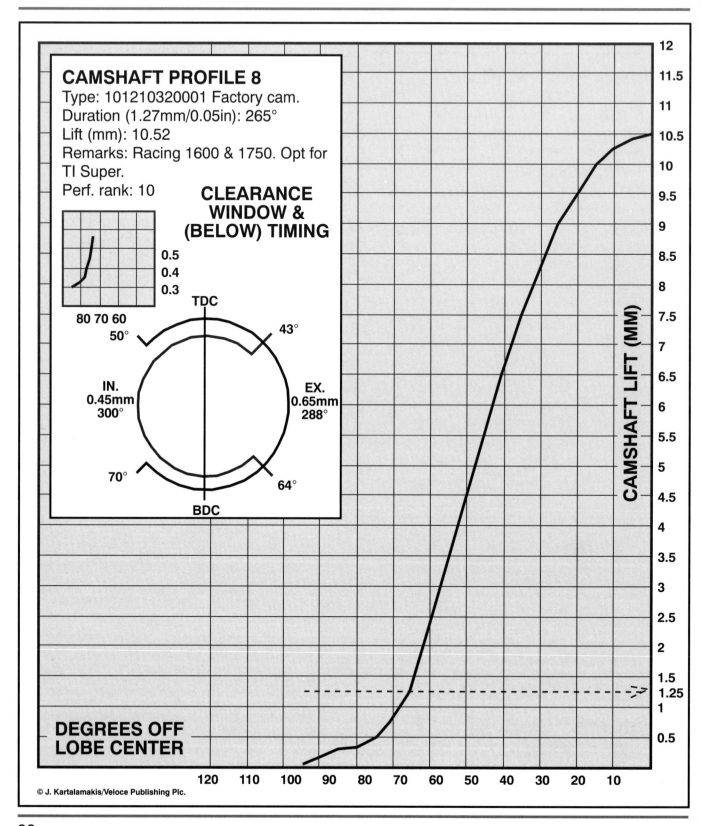

**CAMSHAFT PROFILE 8**
Type: 101210320001 Factory cam.
Duration (1.27mm/0.05in): 265°
Lift (mm): 10.52
Remarks: Racing 1600 & 1750. Opt for TI Super.
Perf. rank: 10

CLEARANCE WINDOW & (BELOW) TIMING

0.5
0.4
0.3

80 70 60
50°

TDC

43°

IN.
0.45mm
300°

EX.
0.65mm
288°

70°

64°

BDC

CAMSHAFT LIFT (MM)

12
11.5
11
10.5
10
9.5
9
8.5
8
7.5
7
6.5
6
5.5
5
4.5
4
3.5
3
2.5
2
1.5
1.25
1
0.5

DEGREES OFF LOBE CENTER

120  110  100  90  80  70  60  50  40  30  20  10

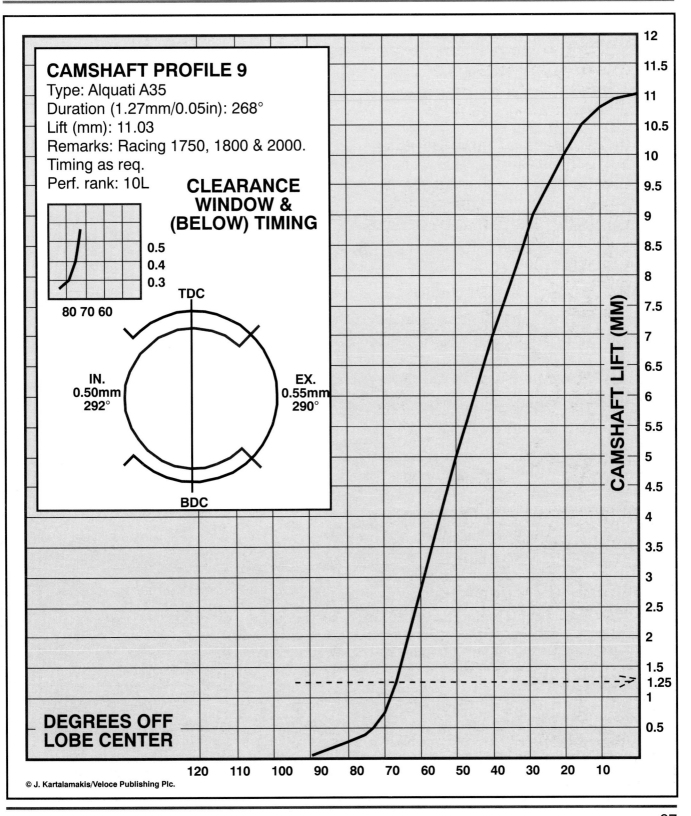

## CAMSHAFT PROFILE 9

Type: Alquati A35
Duration (1.27mm/0.05in): 268°
Lift (mm): 11.03
Remarks: Racing 1750, 1800 & 2000.
Timing as req.
Perf. rank: 10L

**CLEARANCE WINDOW & (BELOW) TIMING**

0.5
0.4
0.3

80 70 60

TDC

IN.
0.50mm
292°

EX.
0.55mm
290°

BDC

**DEGREES OFF LOBE CENTER**

**CAMSHAFT LIFT (MM)**

120   110   100   90   80   70   60   50   40   30   20   10

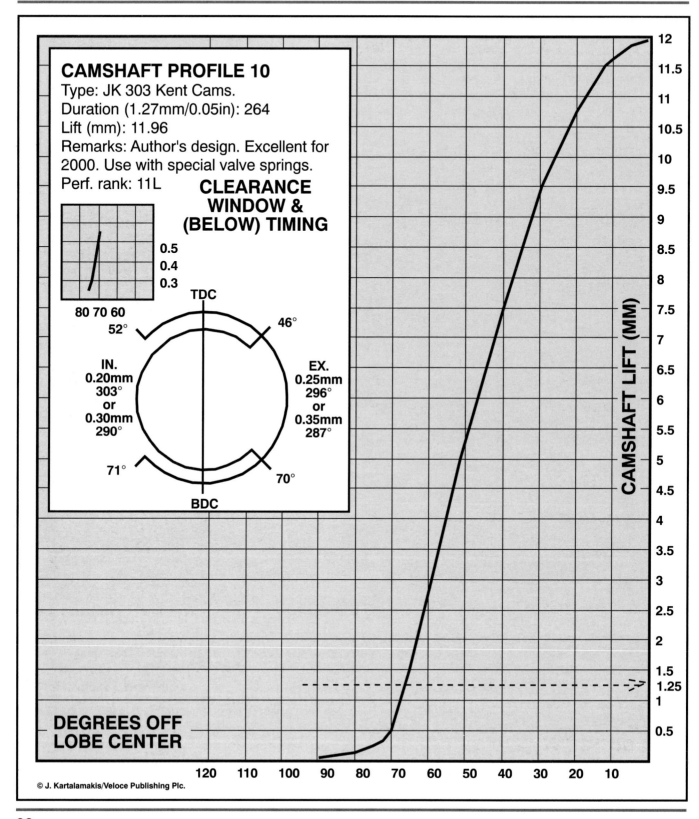

## CAMSHAFT PROFILE 10
Type: JK 303 Kent Cams.
Duration (1.27mm/0.05in): 264
Lift (mm): 11.96
Remarks: Author's design. Excellent for 2000. Use with special valve springs.
Perf. rank: 11L

**CLEARANCE WINDOW & (BELOW) TIMING**

0.5
0.4
0.3

80 70 60

52°

TDC

46°

IN.
0.20mm
303°
or
0.30mm
290°

EX.
0.25mm
296°
or
0.35mm
287°

71°

70°

BDC

CAMSHAFT LIFT (MM)

12
11.5
11
10.5
10
9.5
9
8.5
8
7.5
7
6.5
6
5.5
5
4.5
4
3.5
3
2.5
2
1.5
1.25
1
0.5

**DEGREES OFF LOBE CENTER**

120 110 100 90 80 70 60 50 40 30 20 10

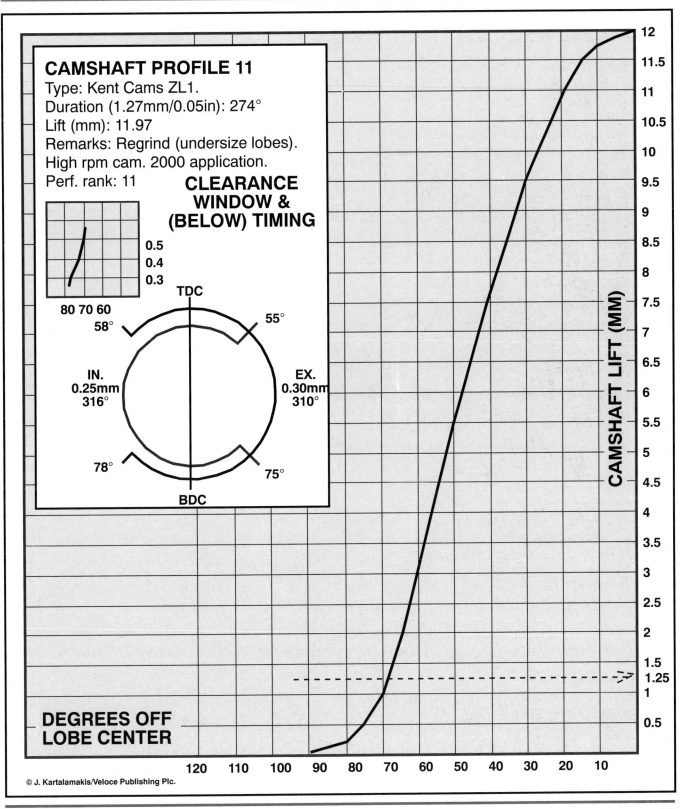

## CAMSHAFT PROFILE 11
Type: Kent Cams ZL1.
Duration (1.27mm/0.05in): 274°
Lift (mm): 11.97
Remarks: Regrind (undersize lobes).
High rpm cam. 2000 application.
Perf. rank: 11

### CLEARANCE WINDOW & (BELOW) TIMING

0.5
0.4
0.3

80 70 60

TDC

58°

55°

IN.
0.25mm
316°

EX.
0.30mm
310°

78°

75°

BDC

**DEGREES OFF LOBE CENTER**

CAMSHAFT LIFT (MM)

12
11.5
11
10.5
10
9.5
9
8.5
8
7.5
7
6.5
6
5.5
5
4.5
4
3.5
3
2.5
2
1.5
1.25
1
0.5

120  110  100  90  80  70  60  50  40  30  20  10

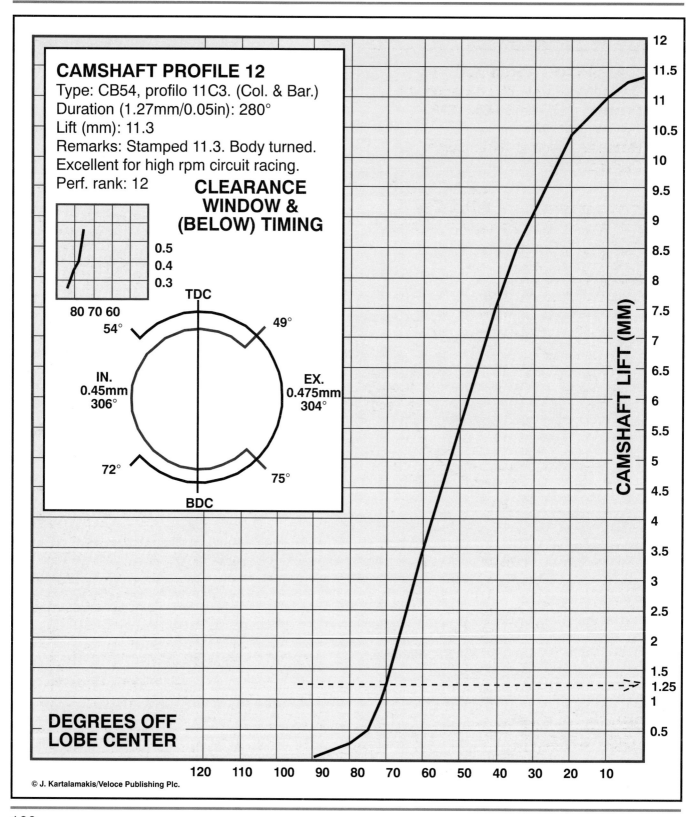

**CAMSHAFT PROFILE 12**
Type: CB54, profilo 11C3. (Col. & Bar.)
Duration (1.27mm/0.05in): 280°
Lift (mm): 11.3
Remarks: Stamped 11.3. Body turned.
Excellent for high rpm circuit racing.
Perf. rank: 12

**CLEARANCE WINDOW & (BELOW) TIMING**

0.5
0.4
0.3

80 70 60
54°

TDC

49°

IN.
0.45mm
306°

EX.
0.475mm
304°

72°

75°

BDC

**DEGREES OFF LOBE CENTER**

CAMSHAFT LIFT (MM)

12
11.5
11
10.5
10
9.5
9
8.5
8
7.5
7
6.5
6
5.5
5
4.5
4
3.5
3
2.5
2
1.5
1.25
1
0.5

120  110  100  90  80  70  60  50  40  30  20  10

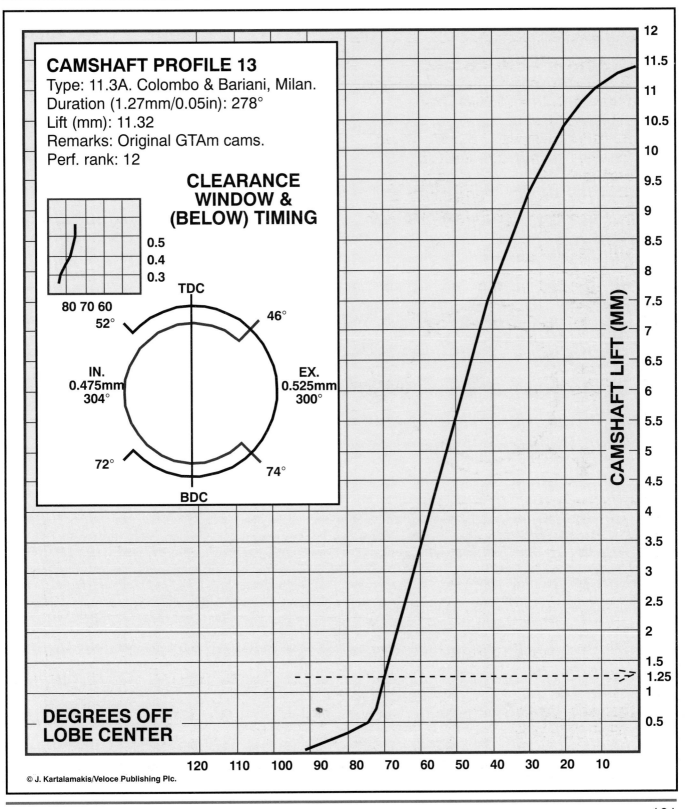

## CAMSHAFT PROFILE 13
Type: 11.3A. Colombo & Bariani, Milan.
Duration (1.27mm/0.05in): 278°
Lift (mm): 11.32
Remarks: Original GTAm cams.
Perf. rank: 12

### CLEARANCE WINDOW & (BELOW) TIMING

0.5
0.4
0.3

80 70 60

TDC
52°      46°
IN.        EX.
0.475mm   0.525mm
304°       300°
72°       74°
BDC

CAMSHAFT LIFT (MM)

**DEGREES OFF LOBE CENTER**

120 110 100 90 80 70 60 50 40 30 20 10

1.25

© J. Kartalamakis/Veloce Publishing Plc.

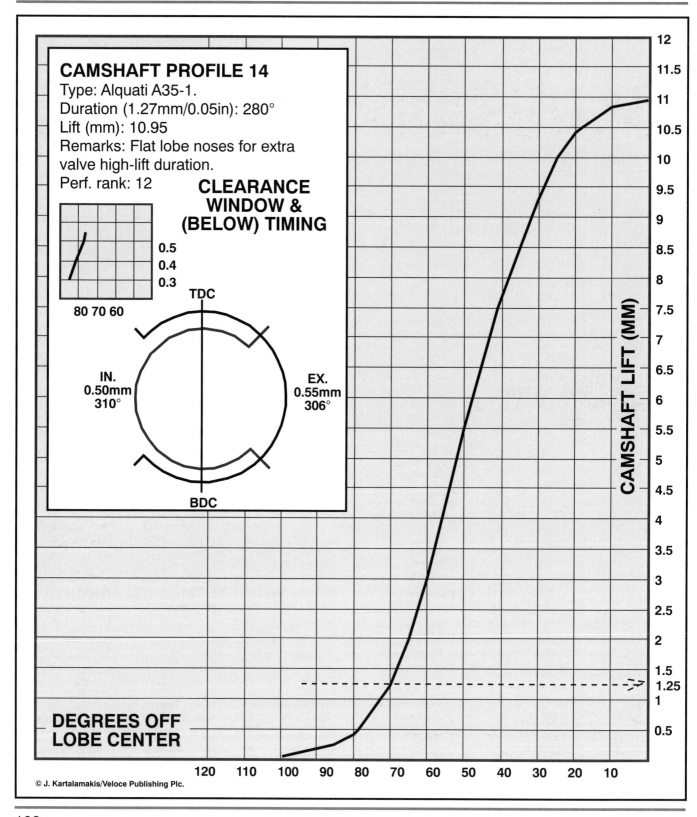

**CAMSHAFT PROFILE 14**
Type: Alquati A35-1.
Duration (1.27mm/0.05in): 280°
Lift (mm): 10.95
Remarks: Flat lobe noses for extra valve high-lift duration.
Perf. rank: 12

**CLEARANCE WINDOW & (BELOW) TIMING**

0.5
0.4
0.3

80 70 60

TDC

IN.
0.50mm
310°

EX.
0.55mm
306°

BDC

CAMSHAFT LIFT (MM)

12
11.5
11
10.5
10
9.5
9
8.5
8
7.5
7
6.5
6
5.5
5
4.5
4
3.5
3
2.5
2
1.5
1.25
1
0.5

**DEGREES OFF LOBE CENTER**

120  110  100  90  80  70  60  50  40  30  20  10

## AMERICAN/ENGLISH GLOSSARY OF AUTOMOTIVE TERMS

| American | English |
|---|---|
| A-arm | Wishbone (suspension) |
| Air horns | Ram pipes |
| Antenna | Aerial |
| Axleshaft | Halfshaft |
| Back-up | Reverse |
| Barrel | Choke/venturi |
| Block | Chock/wedge |
| Box end wrench | Ring spanner |
| Bushing | Bush |
| Clutch hub | Synchro hub |
| Coast | Freewheel |
| Convertible | Drop head |
| Cotter pin | Split pin |
| Counterclockwise | Anti-clockwise |
| Countershaft | Layshaft (of gearbox) |
| Crescent wrench | Open-ended spanner |
| Curve | Corner |
| Dashboard | Facia |
| Denatured alcohol | Methylated spirit |
| Dome lamp | Interior light |
| Drill gun | Electric drill |
| Driveaxle | Driveshaft |
| Driveshaft | Propeller shaft |
| Fender | Wing/mudguard |
| Firewall | Bulkhead |
| Flashlight | Torch |
| Float bowl | Float chamber |
| Freeway, turnpike, etc. | Motorway |
| Frozen | Seized |
| Gas tank | Petrol tank |
| Gas pedal | Accelerator pedal |
| Gasoline (gas) | Petrol |
| Gearshift | Gearchange |
| Generator (DC) | Dynamo |
| Ground | Earth (electrical) |
| Header/manifold | Manifold |
| Heat riser | Hot spot (exhaust) |
| High | Top gear |
| Hood | Bonnet (engine cover) |
| Idle | Tickover |
| Intake | Inlet |
| Jackstands /Safety stands | Axle stands |
| Jumper cable | Jump lead |
| Keeper | Collet |
| Kerosene | Paraffin |
| Knock pin | Roll pin |
| Lash | Freeplay Clearance |
| Latch | Catch |
| Latches | Locks |
| License plate /tag plate | Number plate |
| Light | Lamp |
| Lock (for valve spring retainer) | Split cotter (for valve cap) |

| | | | | | |
|---|---|---|---|---|---|
| Lopes | Hunts | Recap | Retread | Tang or lock | Tab |
| Lug nut | Wheel nut | Release cylinder | Slave cylinder | Taper pin | Cotter pin |
| | | Repair shop | Garage | Teardown | Strip(down) |
| Metal chips | | Replacement | Renewal | | dismantle |
| or debris | Swarf | Ring gear | | Throw-out bearing | Thrust bearing |
| Misses | Misfires | (of differential) | Crownwheel | Tie-rod | |
| Muffler | Silencer | Rocker panel | Sill panel | (or connecting | |
| | | Rod bearing | Big-end bearing | rod) | Trackrod (of |
| Oil pan | Sump | Rotor/disk | Disc (brake) | | steering) |
| Open flame | Naked flame | | | Transmission | Gearbox |
| | | Secondary shoe | Trailing shoe (of | Troubleshooting | Fault finding |
| Panel wagon/van | Van | | brake) | | diagnosis |
| Parking light | Sidelight | Sedan | Saloon | Trunk | Boot |
| Parking brake | Handbrake | Setscrew, | | Tube wrench | Box spanner |
| Piston pin or wrist | | Allen screw | Grub screw | Turn signal | Indicator |
| pin bearing/bush | Small (little) end | Shift fork | Selector fork | | |
| | bearing | Shift lever | Gearlever | Valve lifter | Tappet |
| Piston pin | | | gearstick | Valve lifter or | |
| or wrist pin | Gudgeon pin | Shift rod | Selector rod | tappet | Cam follower or |
| Pitman arm | Drop arm | Shock absorber, | | | tappet |
| Power brake | | shock | Damper/shocker | Valve cover | Rocker cover |
| booster | Servo unit | Snap-ring | Circlip | VOM | |
| Primary shoe | Leading shoe (of | Soft top | Hood | (volt ohmmeter) | Multimeter |
| | brake) | Spacer | Distance piece | | |
| Prussian blue | Engineer's blue | Spare tire | Spare wheel | Wheel cover | Roadwheel trim |
| Pry | Prise (force | Spark plug wires | HT leads | Wheel well | Wheelarch |
| | apart) | Spindle arm | Steering arm | Whole drive line | Transmission |
| Prybar | Crowbar | Stablizer | | Windshield | Windscreen |
| Prying | Levering | or sway bar | Anti-roll bar | Wrench | Spanner |
| | | Station wagon | Estate car | | |
| Quarter window | Quarterlight | Stumbles | Hesitates | | |

# INDEX

## ALSO FROM VELOCE PUBLISHING -

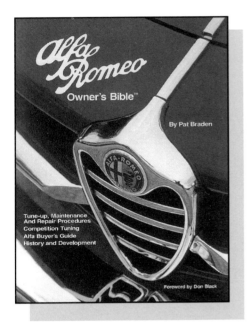

# ALFA ROMEO OWNER'S BIBLE™
## By Pat Braden. Foreword by Don Black

**ISBN 1 874105 45 6**
**£25.00***

## COVERS ALL 1954 ON ALFAS, INCLUDING GIULIETTA • GIULIA • 2600 • ALFETTA

Few cars evoke the passion that comes with owning an Alfa. Like accelerating in 100rpm increments just to hear the harmonious melody of the rising exhaust note. Finding road curves where the tyres bite like newly sharpened ice skates on clean ice. Or lingering over the sensuous body styling and beautiful engine castings - all compound curves and aluminium alloy ...

But it's not always the stuff of high-octane dreams. Alfas can be demanding, frustrating cars to own. They are not inherently unreliable, but can be difficult to understand and troubleshoot when problems arise. The *Alfa Romeo Owner's Bible™* gives you precisely the kind of experienced information you need to happily and confidently buy, maintain and enjoy your Alfa.

Head gasket repairs, valve adjustments, camshaft timing, carburettor and Spica fuel injection tuning and driveshaft doughnut renewal are just a few of the maintenance and repair procedures explained in hands-on fashion and backed up by hundreds of step-by-step illustrations. This tremendously valuable information is crucial to owning, understanding and driving an Alfa - even if you don't work on it yourself.

You'll also get expert advice on the things you should know when buying a used or classic Alfa - specifically, where to look for rust problems, neglect and abuse - plus choosing accessories and fascinating history.

If you own or lust after an Alfa Romeo, this is THE book for you. Over 280 pages of experienced Alfa lore and hands-on advice make sure that you become an Alfa expert and get the very best from your Alfa.

### CHAPTERS
1 Alfa - A Brief History • 2 Your Alfa - A Guided Tour • 3 Buying an Alfa • 4 Maintaining Your Alfa • 5 Engine • 6 Fuel & Ignition • 7 Transmission & Drivetrain • 8 Chassis, Tyres & Brakes • 9 Bodywork & Interior • 10 Electrical System Basics • 11 Performance & Racing Modifications • Appendices: Tools, Clubs & Specialists, Bibliography.

### THE AUTHOR
Pat Braden has owned and maintained more than 50 Alfas and is a current columnist and former editor of *Alfa Owner* magazine.

### SPECIFICATION
Paperback • 280 x 216mm (portrait) • 288 pages • 400 photographs and line illustrations • Book number V045

### RETAIL SALES
Veloce books are stocked by or can be ordered from bookshops and specialist mail order companies. Alternatively, Veloce can supply direct (credit cards accepted).
* Price subject to change.

Veloce Publishing Plc, Godmanstone, Dorset DT2 7AE, England. Tel: 01300 341602/Fax: 01300 341065.

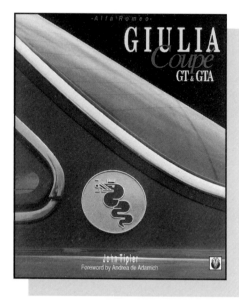

# ALFA ROMEO GIULIA COUPE GT & GTA
## by John Tipler
## Foreword by Andrea de Adamich

**ISBN 1 874105 00 6**
**Price £22.50\***

So popular was Alfa Romeo's Giulia (pronounced *Julia*) Coupe that over 200,000 examples were built between 1963 and 1977. Then, the car converted many to the Alfa cause with its blend of muscular performance and Italian style despite a price tag similar to an E-type Jaguar's! Now, the Giulia Coupe has become a practical and very collectable classic.

Here, at last, is a fact and picture-packed book dedicated solely to the Giulia GT in all its forms including the fabulous lightweight GTA racer. Highly illustrated, the book tells the story of the Giulia from Giugiaro's drawing board to the roads and race tracks of the world. Also included is practical advice from leading experts on buying, restoring and caring for Alfa's classic 'Bertone' coupe together with production figures, road test data, homologation papers, addresses of clubs and specialists, reproductions of contemporary ads and brochure pages and much, much, more.

### CONTENT
FROM ALFA TO GIULIA - Alfa's pre-Giulia history • FROM DRAWING BOARD TO THE WORLD'S SHOWROOMS - Conception, development and production of the Giulia Coupe • THE RACER'S COUPE - The development of the GTA racing versions of the Giulia Coupe • TRACK RECORD - The story of the GT and GTA in International motor racing and rallying • LIVING WITH A GIULIA COUPE - Buying, selling and investment; restoration; spares and repairs; driving experience • ALFA ROMEO MODELS - Alfas in miniature • OFFICIAL PRODUCTION FIGURES • GIULIA COUPE ADVERTISMENTS • SPECIALISTS, CLUBS AND REGISTERS • ROAD TESTS • RADFORD SPRINT GT - A British conversion • HOMOLOGATION PAPERS • SALES BROCHURES.

### THE AUTHOR
John Tipler is a professional motoring journalist who contributes to a number of leading magazines. In the past, John has been Press Officer for John Player Motorsport, worked in the Press Office at Brands Hatch and has been Deputy Editor of the magazine *Restoring Classic Cars*.

### SPECIFICATION
Clothbound hardback • 250x207mm portrait • Artpaper throughout • 160 pages • Over 200 colour, black and white photographs and line illustrations • Book number 006 \* Price subject to change.

### RETAIL SALES
Veloce books are stocked by or can be ordered from bookshops and specialist mail order companies. Alternatively, Veloce can supply direct (credit cards accepted).

\* Price subject to change.

Veloce Publishing Plc, Godmanstone, Dorset DT2 7AE, England. Tel: 01300 341602/Fax: 01300 341065.

## POSTSCRIPT

I hope this book has helped you to build an engine you can be proud of. I hope, too, that my descriptions of some of the more obscure aspects of engine operation may have contributed to your understanding of how power is produced. If this is the case, you should derive even more satisfaction from your car now that you know how, and why, some things are the way they are.

**Jim Kartalamakis**